THE LEGACY OF
DR. LAMAZE

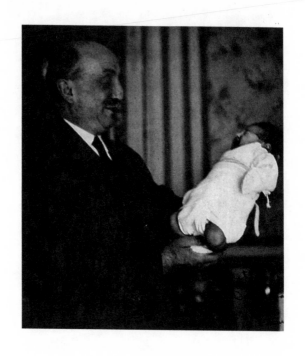

ST. MARTIN'S PRESS
NEW YORK

THE LEGACY OF
DR. LAMAZE

THE STORY OF THE MAN WHO
CHANGED CHILDBIRTH

Caroline Gutmann

Translated by Bruce Benderson

www.stmartins.com

Library of Congress Cataloging-in-Publication Data
Gutmann, Caroline.
    [Testament du Docteur Lamaze. English]
    The legacy of Dr. Lamaze: the story of the man who changed childbirth: a biography/Caroline Gutmann; translated by Bruce Benderson.
        p. cm.
    Includes index.
    ISBN 0-312-26190-X
    1. Lamaze, Fernand, 1890–1957.   2. Obstetricians—France—Biography.   3. Natural childbirth.   4. Pregnancy.   I. Title: Legacy of Doctor Lamaze.   II. Title.

RG76.L35 G8813 2001
618.2'0092—dc21
[B]   2001019274

First published in France under the title *Le Testament du Docteur Lamaze* by Editions Jean-Claude Lattès

First U.S. Edition: August 2001

10   9   8   7   6   5   4   3   2   1

To Anne-Marie, Benjamin, and Jean-Claude

Deserve what you dream.

—OCTAVIO PAZ

Contents

Genealogy

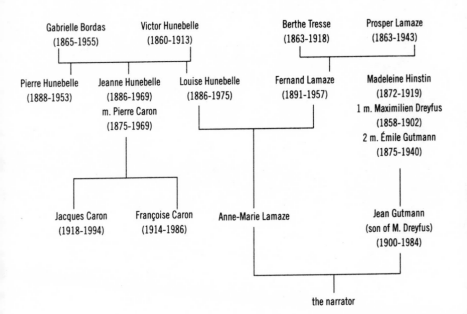

Gabrielle Bordas (1865-1955) — Victor Hunebelle (1860-1913)

Berthe Tresse (1863-1918) — Prosper Lamaze (1863-1943)

Pierre Hunebelle (1888-1953)

Jeanne Hunebelle (1886-1969)
m. Pierre Caron (1875-1969)

Louise Hunebelle (1886-1975)

Fernand Lamaze (1891-1957)

Madeleine Hinstin (1872-1919)
1 m. Maximilien Dreyfus (1858-1902)
2 m. Émile Gutmann (1875-1940)

Jacques Caron (1918-1994)

Françoise Caron (1914-1986)

Anne-Marie Lamaze

Jean Gutmann (son of M. Dreyfus) (1900-1984)

the narrator

Foreword

One day, as I was leaving a reading following the French publication of this book about my grandfather, Fernand Lamaze, a young woman approached me with a broad smile on her lips and a rounded belly that indicated advanced pregnancy. She was American, her name was Mary Burke, and she was, indeed, seven months pregnant. Following in the footsteps of her mother and eldest sister, she had already begun training in the Lamaze Method in the United States, but her husband had recently been sent on special assignment to Paris, and she wanted to finish her course here. The large Parisian hospital she contacted after arriving had merely set up a meeting with the anesthesiologist for the epidural, without seriously considering her request for Lamaze training. "We have childbirth awareness days. Find out about them," she was told. She did, and found herself squeezed like a sardine between two other pregnant women in a packed room while a harried midwife hurriedly explained the mechanisms of childbirth. Both time and means were lacking for more personalized treatment; the medical staff, Mary told me, was doing what it could, but tended to retreat behind technology, that healer of all ills. "There is no danger. Everything is already taken care of—monitoring and epidural—and you'll be able to leave the hospital four days after the delivery." Mary confessed she felt like a number on a file. She had thought France was the country that pioneered painless childbirth, and that on every street corner she would find places where expectant mothers would be guided through the childbirth process, from preparation to delivery, according to Lamaze's precepts. Where were they? she wanted to know.

I wondered what to tell her without destroying her illusions. There are still places in France that use the Lamaze Method of painless childbirth—or *l'accouchement sans douleur,* as it is called in French—but they are few and far between. Judging by the large number of letters I received after my book was published, it seems as if the pendulum may finally swing back toward using the Lamaze Method. Nonetheless, France, the country that invented obstetrics and in essence "medicalized" childbirth, has gradually abandoned its mothers-to-be to the dehumanized world of the hospital. The epidural, deemed a universal cure-all by the medical community, certainly has some value, but it is no substitute for dealing humanely and directly with women's fear and anxiety about labor.

I knew that explaining this contradiction to Mary would take time, so I suggested we have dinner together. We went to a restaurant called Les Papilles, which that evening was offering a Toulousian cassoulet whose delicious aroma put an end to any vague plans I'd had of going on a diet. While waiting for this exquisite dish, I began sketching out the major stages in the history of childbirth in France.

"In sorrow thou shalt bring forth children." For centuries, women have been held hostage to this biblical precept linking the essence of childbirth and suffering to Eve's original sin. This pro-pain view of childbirth is still supported by everyday speech (in French a woman going into labor is said to *entrer en douleurs,* which means roughly "enter the period of pain"). This view was endorsed by most French doctors up to the 1950s, when Lamaze introduced his techniques. Other countries held somewhat different views. In England, for example, in 1853, Queen Victoria asked for chloroform during the birth of her eighth child, thereby making obstetric analgesia acceptable. However, France's Empress Eugenie, who had a forceps delivery three years later, refused all pain relievers. Nonetheless it is to France, I told Mary, that we are indebted for turning childbirth into a medical procedure.

Until the seventeenth century, maternity was a woman's affair and handled by midwives. They guarded their wisdom jealously; secrets of the trade were passed from mother to daughter. There were no fixed rules. Methods varied according to the midwife and the region. In the villages surrounding the southern French city of Montpelier, for example, a woman in labor was made to sit "on the back of a warm cauldron to soften the hind parts." Later, other childbirth positions were advocated: making the woman lie on her back, sit on a chair with a hole in it, stand, or hang from the neck of someone assisting.

Recognizing their validity, François Mauriceau, a surgeon-obstetrician and the author of *Treatise on the Diseases of Pregnant Women and Women in Childbirth* (1668), used midwife techniques in his practice. However, by the eighteenth century, medical expertise would supplant that of midwives.

Childbirth began to be governed by rules that were more and more specific and scientific. For instance, doctors during the Enlightenment believed that the high incidence of child mortality resulted from keeping infants away from their cradles for extended periods. Medical studies increasingly included courses in childbirth, and surgeon-obstetricians subsequently gained power over midwives in Paris (especially those at the famous Hôtel-Dieu medical institute); gradually their influence spread to the provinces.

But the most important figure in obstetrics during this period was a woman. Encouraged first by King Louis XV and then by Louis XVI, Madame du Coudray single-handedly trained more than ten thousand midwives between 1759 and 1783. Traveling from city to city, she taught with the aid of an adjustable mannequin that could simulate the different phases of childbirth (one can still see it on display at the Flaubert Museum in Rouen). Her lessons, which were adopted by professional doctors and accompanied by a manual containing questions and answers, dispensed information about childbirth throughout France.

In 1806 Napoleon gave obstetrics royal authority by appointing Jean-Louis Baudelocque to the Chair of Obstetrics at the Maternity Hospital of Paris, the first medical specialty professorship in France. Ironically enough, Baudelocque was a military man whose efforts at developing the new science were guided by hopes of providing France with future soldiers. Baudelocque's idea was that certified "knowledge" should trickle down to the women actually performing deliveries. Thus he appointed Marie-Louise la Chapelle, a highly respected midwife, to an important position in his practice. By offering courses at every maternity hospital, Baudelocque and his successors significantly improved the professional training of midwives.

In addition to proper training, the prevention of puerperal fever, also called childbed fever or postpartum fever, was the other battlefield in the struggle for obstetric control. The fever had reached such endemic proportions that, until the late nineteenth century, it killed one out of every ten women who went into labor. In 1857, Stéphane Tarnier had devoted a dissertation to the disease, but it was not until 1870 that obstetricians were required to wash their hands before all examinations, or that students coming from autopsies were forbidden to perform obstetric examinations. The strongest case for antisepsis was set forth in 1883 by Adolphe Pinard in *Antiseptic and Obstetrical*

Methodology. Pinard was a brilliant physician and a member of the first graduating class of accredited hospital obstetricians in 1882. When he was appointed to what is now called the Baudelocque Chair in 1889, Pinard revolutionized obstetric science with a paper dealing with "interuterine child care" (1895), which would henceforth become the basis for checkups of pregnant women. During his long career, Pinard proved himself a tireless advocate on all sorts of issues, from pushing for a law that would permit women to take a leave of absence from their jobs while they were pregnant, to courageously opposing a law that outlawed abortion.

In 1914 Alexandre Couvelaire succeeded Pinard, who was his mentor and father-in-law, and continued the fight for antisepsis. Couvelaire, a fervent supporter of raising the birth rate in France, revamped Baudelocque Hospital, creating wings to isolate the tuberculosis patients and the syphilitics (at the time syphilis was responsible for the deaths of twenty thousand children every year). Following the examples of his colleagues, his first concern was to "save the seed" and repopulate France following the devastation of World War I. He thus made the child the priority, even if it meant performing cesarians on dying women.

Yet despite all their efforts, between the two world wars most women still refused to have a baby outside of their homes, fearing both puerperal fever and being associated with maternity hospitals, which were places for "bad girls." Catholic midwives put pregnant women on notice. "A home without a mother is a home in disorder," they warned. "Send the mother to the hospital and the father ends up drinking and debauching. Out-of-home deliveries are a symptom of weakening family values."

Maternity had become a political issue. It was the great duty of every woman to pay "the blood tax." Deserving mothers received bonuses (prizes and medals were awarded to those "advancing the cause of the French family"). In such a climate of patriotism, women's suffering during childbirth largely met with indifference on the part of the medical community. "It's an easy form of suffering; as soon as it's over, you laugh about it" went the saying, revealing that in people's minds childbirth and pain were seen as necessarily and inevitably linked. Pain is indeed useful because it indicates the uterine contractions. But some doctors, including Couvelaire, saw pain as "valorizing" women, endowing them with a "moral beauty that shouldn't be diminished by the sleep of total anesthesia."

By 1950, though modern medicine was making giant steps, obstetrics still had little to offer to ease labor pains. Injecting cocaine into the spinal column or giving shots of morphine-scopolamine led to intoxication and addiction and, most important, diminished contractions. Chloroform, which was used frequently, had little effect, and proved toxic, since its anesthetic effects were passed from mother to child.

In England, thanks to the work of obstetrician Grantly Dick-Read, the concept of childbirth "without fear" had been a topic of research since the 1930s. At the same time, scientists in the Soviet Union had begun to develop the "psychoprophylactic" method. But for all that France had done as a pioneer in the field of obstetrics, it still toed the line on the Judeo-Christian vision of birth and suffering as late as 1950. This was the context in which Lamaze offered his method.

Drawing on Ivan Pavlov's and I. Velvoski's theories regarding conditioned reflexes, Lamaze based his method on the idea that fear of pain during childbirth, inculcated for generations, inevitably created a uterine contraction that was painful. Such pain could be reduced by conditioning, by training women in breathing techniques and in how to assume positions that produced muscular relaxation. These ideas were revolutionary because at the time most women did not truly understand how their bodies worked and believed that childbirth pain was divinely sanctioned. Using the Lamaze Method, they would henceforth learn to control and direct the labor process. "There are no miracles," he wrote, "unless you're referring to magic tricks or subterfuge. The woman learns to give birth as she would learn how to swim, as she has learned to read and write."

To improve upon the Soviet method, Lamaze recommended using "little dog" panting respiration rather than deep breathing. It facilitated expulsion of the newborn. He also brought the father into the labor room and made him an integral part of the birth process. Indeed, expectant fathers were encouraged to attend the preparatory course, which was taught by both an obstetrician and a midwife, who now played a decisive role in the new birthing configuration. Thus, assisted by the father and the medical staff, a woman became an active player; she no longer simply endured childbirth but, in a profound sense, delivered her child herself.

By seeking to make childbirth pain-free, Lamaze played a part in the entire feminist struggle for reproductive rights: family planning, self-reliance, the right to an abortion. His revolutionary method shook the citadels of conformity and tradition; all that was needed now was for them to fall. Others followed in his footsteps, developing new techniques, such as those that focused on the child. These included Dr. Frédéric Leboyer's birth without violence, and "haptonomy," which involves communicating with the fetus by touching the mother's belly.

Today it seems as if medicine has again asserted its predominance. The epidural has excluded all serious consideration of women's fear. But you cannot eliminate anxiety merely by controlling pain. A proposed new law in France threatens to reduce the number of childbirth preparation lessons from eight to five and to lower funding levels, thereby severely diminishing the incomes of midwives. Instead of serving us, technological progress could end up dehumanizing childbirth and taking away women's control over their bodies and over birth.

Poor Mary seemed somewhat depressed by my story. To console her, I gave her the address and phone number of an extraordinary midwife named Chantal Birman, who works at the Clinique des Lilas in Paris. Despite her relative youth, Birman still faithfully applies Lamaze's precepts to her work. Moreover, she is supported by a new generation of obstetricians who refuse to cave in to what she calls "technological totality" and who are as concerned with the psychological care of pregnant women as they are with the delivery itself; they see the two, as Lamaze did, as closely linked.

I am also grateful to Birman because through her I was able to contact a friend of my grandfather to whom before his death Lamaze had given a diary of his second trip to the Soviet Union in 1955. The diary contains a number of disturbing revelations, particularly about the highly charged politics surrounding childbirth, family planning, and abortion.

Mary thanked me for the recommendation, then began to ask me more personal questions about my husband and son. What I told her about my husband, Jean-Claude, made her laugh. Jean-Claude has that effect on people. He has a doctorate in linguistics from the University of Strasbourg, is a specialist on the relationship between film and literature, and is currently an editor at a publishing house, but he chose the wrong career. He should have been a comic actor. He's an amazing mimic, and his Donald Duck imitation is in especially high demand.

My son, Benjamin, inherited a good share of his father's talent as a clown. Being eight, he tries to rival his dad but has a long way to go.

I told Mary about the day of his birth, and of my rebirth, when they placed this tiny being so full of life on my belly and I watched in amazement while he tried to haul himself up to my breast. (Benjamin has always been a glutton and would sell his soul to the devil for candy.) This miraculous moment eclipsed the memory of a rather unsuccessful childbirth: I hadn't been "prepared," and the epidural proved only around 75 percent effective, as is frequently the case. As the old saying goes, the baker's children are often the ones who go without bread. It was my own fault. At the time, I didn't want people to know that I was Lamaze's granddaughter, and, over the objections of my mother, who had recommended I consult a doctor she saw as one of her father's spiritual descendants, I went to the big hospital near my home; it was reputed to have the best equipment. From a medical point of view, Benjamin's birth went fine, and I have only praise for the hospital and its staff and their treatment of newborns. Yet I felt let down that they didn't take into account the mother's strong emotions, her capacity to learn to master pain and control her body. In great part this explains my motives for beginning to look into Lamaze's story, and for writing this book.

Today Mary is back in the United States. Her delivery went beautifully, thanks to Chantal Birman. She named her little girl Louise, in honor of my grandmother, Lamaze's wife. They are waiting for me to come visit, but on one condition: that we reverse the roles this time and that I come when I am pregnant. Their family obstetrician, Dr. Andrew Marchal, has reserved me a place in his hospital in New Jersey. All I have to do is give them three months' notice. Perhaps then I will have a chance to see what legacy my grandfather has left in America.

INTRODUCTION

Destiny is character.

—NOVALIS

Family Photographs and a Letter

I NEVER KNEW FERNAND LAMAZE, but I was brought up with his legend.

When I was a little girl, I used to make regular visits to my maternal grandmother, Louise, who had kept the apartment she lived in with Fernand on rue du Dragon in Paris. A victim of myopathy, which was gradually paralyzing her limbs, she was confined to her bed and consumed by the memory of her dear husband. When she spoke of him, she seemed to shine with such happiness that no one would have suspected any problems in their marriage.

On the wall of her room were two photos of my grandfather. One showed him a year before his death in 1957, receiving the Medal of the City of Saint-Denis and the Union of French Women; in the other he is signing his book on his method of painless childbirth before a crowd of young workers, while at his side my grandmother, wearing a small black hat with a veil, beams in admiration.

Both photos give an impression of tranquillity and power from Lamaze, with his large body, rounded forehead, and patriarchal beard. He looks as if he would have made a good grandfather.

The first ten years of my life were spent before the shrine of a man I had never known. My grandmother slowly faded away, becoming more luminous the more her body atrophied; then one day she passed away and the doors of the rue du Dragon were shut to me forever. An absurd kind of sentimentality made me avoid that childhood street for years. I made every effort not to have to walk in the neighborhood or cross into what felt like forbidden territory. When, much later, I decided to go back, I did not at first recognize the little street, which had lost its provincial charm and been transformed into a vast garment bazaar. I found the change strangely comforting. My rue du Dragon lay preserved and concealed under yards of fabric.

Though I heard Lamaze's name from time to time in the world— usually because his method was under attack for political reasons, which disturbed me but left me feeling helpless—he remained frozen in my memory, as imposing and rigid as the marble statue over his grave in the cemetery in the little town of Grosrouvre, outside Paris. Then, gradually, the statue began to come to life.

The process started with some photographs. I was an only child of parents without ties, and therefore missed out on those noisy and troublesome family reunions, the kind where loyalties often mask deep resentment. I dreamed about family connections—about uncles, aunts, and distant cousins—but by the time I had grown up I was accustomed to my isolation. Then one day I happened to come across a stack of faded photos at the back of a desk in my mother's apartment on rue du Cherche-Midi. Someone had written the names on the back in purple ink, and they immediately seemed familiar to me: Aunt Lolotte, Jean Bordas, Gabrielle Hunebelle, Blanche Selva. And among them was my grandfather's sharp, hard face, looking somehow out of place.

I had gone to my mother's apartment to get some of her belongings, following her hospitalization for what is euphemistically termed a nervous breakdown. Perhaps because of that, suddenly coming across images of her forgotten family seemed that much more significant and poignant.

The photographs fell into two distinct groups: those of the Hunebelles and those of the Lamazes. My maternal grandmother's family, which descended from the three Hunebelle brothers, famous for having constructed France's central railroad network as well as creating its sewer system, seem strikingly elegant and self-assured. My great-great-grandfather Victor sets the tone. There is a photo of him in Mauritius surrounded by luxurious vegetation; he is wearing white trousers and smoking a pipe, his eyes concealed beneath the brim of a pith helmet. At his feet is a basket containing two babies: my grandmother Louise and her twin sister, Jeanne. Then, a few years later, he is in the garden of his *hôtel particulier* (private residence) on rue Pierre-Nicole. He has entered the new century with an air of nonchalance and self-assurance, despite the reversals in fortune that nearly ruined the family and were apparently caused by his notorious incompetence. The only thing clouding the sense of prosperity and ease of this man in the twilight of his life was the rheumatism detectable in his clenched hands. At his side is Aunt Lolotte, a well-known singer and, from what I am told, certified nuisance, somewhat grimly holding the arm of Maurice Bonhomme, her husband and one of the founders of the Renault car industry. Another picture shows Aunt Jules, the ex-mistress of former French president Paul Doumer, talking with the twin girls. Aunt Jules was infamous for her incorrigible kleptomania and her untrustworthiness.

In a photograph taken by the legendary photographer Gaspard-Félix Tournachon Nadar, Louise and Jeanne are pictured side by side, their waists pinched by white taffeta dresses, looking eerily alike, as though bonded by some hidden force. I often wondered whether one dominated the other, as happens with most twins. Then there was a photo showing my grandmother dressed as a man; she is wearing a lacy ascot, looking both forward and innocent, and visibly ill-at-ease. Next were photos of my mother, Anne-Marie. I found them disturbing; each one seems to project a different personality: the light-hearted little girl, the rebellious adolescent, the daring young woman bending toward the camera lens, her hair awry, laughing and showing her breasts.

Lamaze's family never would have been allowed to laugh during a photo session. Packed into heavy woolen clothing, sparing in their gestures, the Lamazes seem distinctly ill at ease in a photography studio. You can read the toil and sweat in this family of peasants from the Lorraine region in eastern France, near the border with Germany (and always disputed territory), and their pride at having hoisted themselves up by their own bootstraps to become teachers. Prosper, my grandfather's father, is the product of their upward mobility. Looking like a wizened farmer, he is pictured at the head of a class of provincial schoolchildren, wearing clogs and black blouses. Next to him stands Fernand, looking like a runt because of his pallor and enormous shaved skull. Prosper, a man of order and habit, projected all his hopes onto his son, urging him to take the high road of national service and to avoid the side streets. Prosper hoped Fernand would follow in his footsteps and become a teacher, perhaps even— who knew?—an inspector at a teacher's college. He would help spread the message about public schools. In another photograph, wearing a sailor's suit, Fernand is looking at his pocketwatch. What his father couldn't know is that his son dreamed of a different destiny, one that would involve not teaching children about the world but bringing them into the world.

There was a photograph of Fernand during the Great War—as World War I is called in Europe—when he served as a field medic.

He is lying in the grass, surrounded by his comrades-in-arms, looking like a doomed man. Bearded and undernourished, he has the eyes of someone who has been a silent witness to slaughter. Perhaps it was the charnel house of that war that convinced him to dedicate his life to making life better—to making it "painless."

The next series of photographs shows him almost half a century later, looking triumphant, holding babies in his arms or sitting at the bedside of their mothers, each one smiling and looking relaxed. These photographs conform to the image I had of him: a courageous man of the people who tenaciously scaled the summits of the medical world and devoted his life to women's struggles.

A small black-and-white photo happened to fall from the batch. Taken in 1952, in the country, it shows Lamaze seated at a table with friends, his arm around a woman whose face has been blackened out with ink. She cannot be my grandmother Louise; the svelte body suggests a much younger woman. Something in Lamaze's expression bothers me. Perhaps it is the hard look in his eyes—mischievous, triumphant, and ironic; it reveals something I had not known before. Suddenly I felt like a stranger stealing secrets to which I had no right. I closed the drawer.

My mother's room at Montsouris Hospital opened to a small garden, where she went every afternoon to rest. She had become acquainted with two other patients: "Andrée," a chronic depressive who had recently made her second suicide attempt and who was having a go at electroshock after being on lithium for ten years; and "Véronique," a more worldly woman who had ended up at Villa Montsouris after several fruitless stays at more expensive private spas in the Paris area. Whenever I could get away from the office, I joined them for tea, which was characterized by fixed expressions and trembling hands clenching paper cups.

I had not yet dared talk to my mother about the photos I had discovered, nor about my growing interest in her father. It did not seem like the right time. Instead, for the moment, I settled for simply being there with her, as anxious to depart as I had been to arrive. I always felt nervous and at loose ends after leaving her. What I needed, I thought, was a project, something on which to focus my energies. After one tea with my mother, I decided I would go back to her apartment and put her affairs in order.

Following my grandmother's death, some of the papers and documents in her apartment on the rue du Dragon had been thrown out. The rest were transferred to my mother, who simply crammed these photographs, letters, marriage and death certificates, and diaries—the traces of our brief passage through this world—into drawers and cabinets. Nobody ever bothered to look at them. They were just there to vouch for the family memory. I began my work by looking only at the official-looking documents, which I placed in colored folders; the temptation to read the letters was strong, yet I resisted it. But as the days passed and my mother's hospital stay lengthened, I gave in to that temptation. I wanted to explore the world that they opened up to me.

Buried at the bottom of a drawer I discovered a letter my grandfather had written to Jean Le Bey Taillis, a schoolmate from Nancy, the city in the Lorraine where he was born. Lamaze's letter had obviously never reached his friend. Le Bey Taillis was also the person to whom Lamaze dedicated a thick gray notebook entitled *Ramblings,* a collection of very amateurish and self-conscious literary jottings— the dreams of a young man from the sticks dying to conquer Paris. Written in a small, delicate, and nervous hand, the letter gave me a place to start:

August 28, 1910

My Friend,

My member came out of the cathouse in a great mood, but my heart is at half-mast. Since it's my last night in Nancy I went there to celebrate with the city sluts in houses that smell of old leather and sour urine. I'm going to miss the Lorraine, with its flat horizon, its houses molded from mud and manure, and its whores with eyes lit up by rosé.

At the end of the day, I wanted to stop in and see your mother. As usual, she was at the back of her workshop, painting. She seemed so absorbed in her work that she didn't notice me and I tiptoed away, without one word of good-bye to the woman I owe everything.

Returning to reality seemed that much more brutal. The Café de la Rotonde was packed with old men who looked like sextons, sly and horny, drinking cold beers with ladies who were less so. They'd all left the rue des Moulins to grab a client as night fell. An almost gypsylike orchestra was wearing itself out, banging out the latest waltzes from Vienna. It wasn't a pretty sight, and after a few glasses, I left for a final venereal workout in the city of our loves.

My crude language offends you. Your principles stick to your skin like eczema patches, so you keep dreaming of a great love. And so did I, wandering the shores of the Moselle, burning with some mystic fire. Under the moon, the chalky parapets whitened the river with vague reflections of metal, and I could hear the water murmuring on the pebbly banks. That was where I composed my sublime poems, desperate verses about the Eternal Woman, but that time is over. My peach fuzz has been replaced by a heavy beard, shameful pimples now redden my poet's forehead, so one fine day I decided to shake the mud off my shoes and go looking for my soul mate in the whorehouse on rue des Moulins.

The "34" is quite an honorable establishment, run by your better type of madam who thinks Bourget's naughty. This Mme Lethu, who runs the place, is so fat that she can't get out of her chair, which is shaped like a cathedral. So she has time to read. To the rhythm of her clients' diddlings she drones out some of today's great literary works. She does it so well that you can't shoot your wad and make it to the exit without having to deal with the highly philosophical considerations of that ancient bird plastered in so much foundation and rouge that it makes her look almost like something from a horror story. Yet isn't satisfying your organ worth a few concessions?

Say, do you remember Sylvie, daughter of the gamekeeper of the woods in Portieux? You and I were so worked up over that angelic face and that look of a knowing nymphet we were on the brink of a duel. Her father was honest enough to tell anybody who'd listen that his daughter wasn't the "available type" and had better plans than marrying some guy from the village. Well, guess what? Now our Sylvie spends her time offering her randy white flesh to the rough hands of soldiers in Nancy. What a sad fate! A slightly absurd sentimentality kept me from giving in to her advances, and I chose a little brunette with big tits to spend the night with.

Monique—that's her name—was quite a pro, and I came out of that cathouse as straddled as an old stallion. The young lady was kind enough to propose a little walk and we went out to explore the city, arm in arm like a couple of old lovers.

The two bottles of red she'd downed were making my fiancée a little tipsy, her rough flannel dress clung crudely to her low-slung ass. I was a little ashamed to be wandering around the Stanislas area like this, with a whore, but it was cold and dark and I needed to feel a little human warmth.

The more we sank into those tortuous backstreets of old Nancy, the more the memories flooded my mind and my chest tightened with a melancholy feeling. Those snail-hunting parties and fishing for crayfish with Grandfather were over forever. What would happen to that sweet, disciplined education I'd received as a child, and the man who'd initiated me into nature's mysteries and the subtleties of the old local patois jokes? And what about my mother Berthe? Would she be able to drown her boredom in enough alcohol to stand her punctilious husband?

On rue de Maure-qui-Trompe, the odor of greasy sauerkraut made me gag and kept me from dwelling on old memories. Couples were entwined under the lamplights wrapped in blue paper. This "bucolic" atmosphere made Monique talkative. Between hiccups, in a tremulous voice, she told me about her future plans, the money she'd so bitterly put away, the eligible catch who'd taken so long to come. She would be a good housewife, devoted body and soul to her husband and his offspring, which she hopes will be numerous. The tale of such a limited life took us to the Neptune fountains and the amphitheater, where, coward that I am, I let my protégée sink into a drunken sleep.

Under the black starless sky of the Lorraine, I think of the marvelous stability of Stanislas Place. Nothing here can change. The horizon will forever remain flat, the houses, over their doors a whitewashed cross, never change.

Is it the fantasy of another life calling me to Paris? I want it to be shimmering and sordid at the same time, as in those Jean Lorrain novels we used to read. As a pledge to our friendship, I took the pipe you brought back from Cairo. It will keep me from becoming bourgeois and from looking like those provincial lawyers who only know how to spell their name and count their salary!

I'm waiting for lots of letters from you at the Institute for the Deaf and Dumb, 254 rue Saint-Jacques. That's where I'll be each night, emptying pots of urine and vomit, so that I can feed my mind on the precepts of Charcot's descendants during the day. That way I hope to finish my studies in neurology without my father's help and come back old and venerable to the land of my childhood. Then I'll savor my last years tranquilly contemplating the bordered landscape of the Moselle with its delicate waters and monotonous banks, behind which the same sun sinks every evening.

Your faithful friend,
Fernand

Besides the various biographical details and idle thoughts about existence, the letter offered me something tangible—Lamaze's whereabouts in the fall of 1910: 254 rue Saint-Jacques. I lived only a few steps away from that address, the location of the famous eighteenth-century school founded by Charles Michel, Abbé de l'Epée, dedicated to the study of the Eustachian tube: the world-famous Institute for the Deaf and Dumb.

"Are you the one doing research on Abbé Rousselet's phonetic language laboratory?"

This was the question put to me a few days later by a little man with brown hair and a bristly mustache. It pulled me out of the pleasant daydream I had sunk into while waiting for the document librarian in the institute's courtyard. The man had planted himself directly in front of me and obviously expected an answer. His neck was squeezed into a shirt with a heavily starched collar; large drops of sweat were running down his forehead, which he nervously sponged with a thick, yellow-checked handkerchief. Given his air of self-importance, I figured he had to be the librarian I had come to see, a certain Albéric Lillet.

I wondered how I could keep from disappointing the poor man, who had clearly been waiting for someone else. No, I told him, the Abbé Rousselet's language laboratory was not part of my current field of research. I invented a scholarly identity that was as pompous as it was vague, and this seemed momentarily to satisfy his curiosity. He politely invited me to cross the courtyard. We struggled up the steep stairway leading to the library. I took my time, frantically trying to concoct some reasonable excuse for taking up his time.

At the top of the stairs, I had a sudden impulse to turn back, but M. Lillet was already delivering up the treasures of his archives.

I had been to a number of archival libraries in Paris during my school years. Each has its own discreet charm, and each one attracts its own following: Sainte-Geneviève with its students in search of gallant adventures; Mazarine, with its historical maps and tracts, drawing aging cartographers; the theater collection at the Arsenal, with its sentimental, second-rate actresses looking for notices and reviews of their performances; the Paris Opera archives, with its clientele of elderly men and women seeking mementos of the heroes and heroines of their youth. Each archive attracts its fair share of harmless cranks, widows, and retirees, each working on a memoir or biography that stands little or no chance of ever being published, or seeking some clue from the past before they, too, join the dust covering the papers and books.

I was therefore ready for anything as I pushed open the door of the library at the Institute of the Deaf and Dumb, but I had not expected to find myself in a linen room. M. Lillet serenely explained that the room was the most comfortable and well lit in the entire building and therefore an ideal place to store boxes from the archives. After a while, he added, one got used to the comings and goings of workers pushing carts piled high with sheets and towels for patients.

Trying to remain composed, I followed M. Lillet to a table at the far end of the room, where two studious-looking researchers—obviously accustomed to the room's oddities—were hard at work. One was a young American linguist writing a paper on Abbé Sicard, the other a retired biologist interested in the history of medicine.

The moment of truth had arrived. Out of my bag I took a sheet of paper and a capless pen (I always lose the caps) and turned to face M. Lillet. What rationale would I give him? That I wanted to research the history of sign language? Examine writing samples by children who were deaf and dumb? I told him that I was undertaking a sociological study involving the teaching and domestic staff in specialized institutions in Paris at the turn of the century.

The half-smile M. Lillet gave me indicated that he thought my request a legitimate one. He headed off, and I sat down at the table to wait. Before long, carts of documents were brought to me in boxes.

I began with the ones labeled *Subordinate*—involving drivers, delivery boys, laundry workers, maids, and bursars who worked at the institute during the time in question—and soon learned a great deal about their daily life: salary, food, clothes, even how the institute graciously paid for their shoes to be resoled twice each year. Lamaze's name was not mentioned in the files. I therefore dove into the boxes labeled *Secondary*—involving the teaching and professional staff—and slogged through lengthy descriptions of the epidemics of scarlet fever, diphtheria, ringworm, and other illnesses they periodically had to deal with.

After skimming three entire folders devoted exclusively to the ailments suffered by a class of young children who had eaten rotten lentils, I finally came upon a large notebook listing, by year, the names of the on-call staff. I rushed to the year 1910 and scanned the twenty-seven names I found there. My grandfather's wasn't among them. I wondered whether he had worked at the institute under another name. Perhaps, I thought, he had been in a personnel category deemed unworthy of mention in the registers.

I asked M. Lillet about the completeness of these sources. He replied dryly that you could never be certain of anything and that there were probably other documents somewhere in the basement. He told me that if I wanted to do a more exhaustive search, he would communicate my request to the management.

I had spent the entire day without finding a thing. By now it was 6:30 P.M.; the library would close in fifteen minutes. The American and the biologist had already left. Behind his impeccably neat desk, M. Lillet sat, fingering his mustache, waiting for the bell that would liberate him from his labors until the next day. Without much hope, I took out the last bundle of documents. They consisted of letters addressed to the institute's director at the turn of the century, Ladreit de la Charrière, and written by the substitute chaplain. The poor man was complaining about an unending series of humiliations inflicted upon him every day by people with an "obviously warped sense of humor": broken thermometers, holy water replaced by urine, and other naughty tricks. Moreover, with what were clearly finely honed detective skills, the chaplain offered the director several hypotheses as to the identity of the "miscreant." There followed a list of those presumed guilty, each amplified by a psychological and moral description of their character, or lack thereof.

Halfway through this rather juicy file, I stumbled upon the following: "After what we have learned from little Lison's confession, we had better review the case of the young attendant Lamaze right away. He represents the kind of element that impedes the good workings of the establishment. For his health and ours, it would be best to separate him as quickly as possible from the souls he is trying to pervert."

What I read opened up to me the world of my grandfather's youth. Closing my eyes, I could see him as a lanky nineteen-year-old. Fernand was before me, not as a legend, but as flesh and blood.

PART ONE

THE OUTSIDER
IN PARIS

The Institute

WHEN HE MOVED INTO the Institute for the Deaf and Dumb on the evening of November 7, 1910, Fernand Lamaze felt strangely uneasy, though he would admit that everything had gone according to plan. The director was both a little condescending and cordial—appropriate in the relations between a supervisor and a subordinate. Fernand was immediately shown to the dormitory; it would be his job to keep an eye on the fifty or so students between 8:30 in the evening and 5:30 in the morning. He patted his cot; it was firm but not hard. The location of the building was ideal for his purposes—near the medical school, in other words. He was deeply impressed by its great historical significance: it had been built on the very site of the former residence of the renowned commander of Saint-Jacques du Haut-Pas and next door to the church that housed the bones of the great Saint Magloire. Fernand knew his French history, and here he was living in it. Last, and most important, this night job would pay fairly well, helping him meet medical school expenses.

Despite all this, Fernand was still uneasy. Perhaps it had something to do with the moans and strange guttural sounds the little deaf-mutes made in their sleep. During his first night at the institute, he had been awakened several times and gone out to investigate. He had stared at the distorted faces of children, awake or asleep, vainly trying to communicate. Unable to get back to sleep, he had gotten up again, drenched in sweat, feeling as though he could not breathe. A child had wet his bed and was crying. Fernand changed the sheets and held the child until he quieted down. The dormitory reeked of disinfectant and urine. Fernand moved unsteadily toward the window, each step making the floor creak and sending up a small cloud of dust. Over the beds hung large crucifixes, which didn't manage to hide the cracks in the walls. Everywhere was misery and austerity. He looked outside.

The buildings of the institute looked majestic in the moonlight. The hundred-foot-high elm, planted in the courtyard by the monks of Saint-Magloire in 1572, scattered the light along the walls. Fernand felt intensely that he was out of his element. He ought never have come to this strange, hostile world. He should have stayed home and become a humble teacher like his father. Here, even the silence was different—it had a different weight and density, enfolding sounds that could not be heard, only felt. The clock had not yet struck four, and the night seemed endless.

Suddenly Fernand heard footsteps in the courtyard below and peered down into the darkness. A shadow appeared at the door to the church and then disappeared behind the elm. He wondered if it were an optical illusion brought on by exhaustion. Who could possibly be out there at this time of night? Moments passed, until again he heard the sound of gravel being crunched underfoot. The door of the penitentiary wing of the institute, the place where problem students or patients were housed, opened with a creak. A figure hurried inside.

At five in the morning, the clock tower tolled, the signal for the staff to wake up and begin the day. A few minutes later the students were awakened by vibrations in the floor. Fernand felt exhausted by his nearly sleepless night. The children seemed restless and got dressed quickly, with large, abrupt movements, under the watchful eye of M. Rodolphe, the floor supervisor.

"Hey, you, stop daydreaming. Get moving or you'll miss prayers."

Fernand turned, surprised by the voice. It belonged to a young woman, barely eighteen, her face half covered by badly cut bangs. She was dressed like a streetwalker in a pleated black skirt and red blouse that was opened to reveal her tiny breasts.

Her name, he learned, was Mlle Lison, a maid who had been working at the institute for a year. Her impish face and sharp tongue, rare for girls in her situation, had earned her the reputation among the kitchen staff of being "quite the spicepot," despite her bad teeth, raw-looking bones, and sallow complexion.

She moved behind Fernand's bed, ripped off the sheets, and began to shake them out. She gave off a musky odor that made his head throb. Her "fallen woman" gaze was focused on this hayseed student supervisor staring at her, his mouth agape.

"Stop staring at me as if I were naked."

Beet-red, Fernand confusedly lowered his head and hurried out of the dormitory, hoping that M. Rodolphe hadn't noticed the encounter.

The children were assembled in the hallway leading to the cafeteria, standing before the chaplain. Gesticulating and grimacing, they were engaged in the curious spectacle of praying together in sign language.

Feeling awkward, Fernand stayed to one side, until the abbot motioned him over to join the group. Then the abbot began to speak in unctuous tones, translating the hand gestures for the new arrival.

Fernand was instinctively uncomfortable in the company of this man. With his wide square shoes and threadbare cassock, he conformed to the image of a country priest. But something about his prying, insinuating eyes reminded you that the habit did not always make the monk.

"It is a great pleasure to welcome among us Fernand Lamaze, who has the difficult job of watching over you while you sleep. His duty will be to monitor you right up to the moment of your dreams and to keep evil away from them.

"Not being able to hear does not shelter you from sin, and you have special needs in terms of instruction in the truths of the catechism. It is God you must listen to, and if you can't hear with your ears, your heart will do the job for you."

A great believer in his own rhetoric, the abbot carefully enunciated his words, accentuating the strong points with his little chubby hands, which he used with the virtuosity of an orchestra conductor. Fernand noticed that his manicured nails were painted pink.

"And now we come to serious matters," the priest continued in his syrupy, monotonous voice. "You know how important I think discipline is, since it especially ensures your soul's salvation.

"Truly, as a tiny army in the service of God, you must obey the rules with military rigor. Each section of the class is a squadron with its own corporal. Every class has its sergeant. And I, your humble commandant, will guide your steps, direct your actions, uplift your soul. What happens when a grain of sand jams the works of that lovely machine devoted to God? Chaos follows, fiasco rules, and the Devil enters through the cracks of disorder.

"Yesterday evening, one of you had escaped my vigilance and refused to comply with the punishments I had meted out to him in the privacy of the confessional. There were no marks on his white body, despite his claiming to have followed my precepts and inflicted penitence on himself, morning and evening. Physical pain is still the only way to stamp out sin and steady the soul. By disobeying, your peer allowed himself to be taken over by evil. But he also put you in peril, especially since, I repeat, the least infraction shatters divine harmony and engenders evil.

"I've reflected deeply about which sanctions to adopt. I could have been easy on the guilty one by depriving him of recreation and walks, put him on bread and soup, or imposed the cure of silence. But gangrene is highly dangerous and can't be permitted to spread. That's why I've decided to separate the subversive element from you for a specified period.

"Blaise, you know whom I'm talking about. Leave your little friends and follow me."

A young boy in a gray shirt crept forward, pale with fear.

He had a helmet of blond curls, an extremely delicate face. More than one young girl would have envied his translucent skin, his wide violet eyes, and the dimple in his chin that gave him a mischievous air.

"Come here, Blaise. Don't be afraid. I do not wish you any harm."

The terrified child raised his head and fixed his eyes on the chaplain, who smilingly caressed his hair. Then he placed his thick hand on the boy's shoulder and gently pushed him toward the exit. Impelled by the priest's massive silhouette, the child seemed resigned to his fate. With tiny steps he left the room, never looking back.

Lamaze remembered the ogres and elves that had peopled his childhood. With a sickening feeling in his stomach, he watched them disappear into the darkness of the corridor.

The First Day

BY 7:30 A.M., NEARLY A HUNDRED students had crowded into the courtyard of Paris's École de Médecine on rue des Écoles. The hours and subjects of this year's courses and labs were to be posted in the entrance hall at 8:00 sharp.

Having performed brilliantly in physics, chemistry, and the natural sciences as a student in Nancy, Fernand felt ready to compete with his Parisian counterparts. At last he was to enter that temple of progress about which he'd dreamed for so long.

The students had already broken into cliques. They were greeting each other jocularly, giving each other noisy hugs, radiating that feeling of well-being that comes with confronting a familiar face. Fernand wandered among the groups, his black satchel pressed to his body, not knowing how exactly to behave. He felt clumsy and self-conscious among these well-dressed young people who had been brought up in an entirely different milieu from his. They revealed social superiority in subtle ways: their negligent way of dressing, the fresh complexion that comes from a regular diet, that distinct way of marking territory they feel belongs to them.

Within minutes Fernand's courage had melted away and the effects of a sleepless night returned in full force. He was but a penniless hick among the future medical elite. He could read the self-satisfaction on their faces. They already seemed to have everything worked out: their future medical specialty (whichever was most lucrative); marriage to the daughter of the boss (preferably an expert in said chosen specialty); the wealthy clientele that would follow from that marriage; and, to top off a life of devotion to themselves, a handsome red lapel ribbon from the Legion of Honor.

It was nearly 8:00. Tension was mounting. The classroom doors were about to open; everyone was jostling for position. No one was standing next to Fernand; it was as if they were afraid to get too close to this large man with his badly shaved beard, muscular shoulders, and gruff air. Perhaps they sensed his inner determination, his obstinacy about pursuing his goals, whatever the consequences.

The proctor had hardly opened the doors when the students poured en masse into the entrance hall and feverishly sought their names on the large blackboard that covered nearly a whole section of the wall.

Fernand looked in consternation at the extent of knowledge he was supposed to acquire in only four years: Anatomy, Histology, and Pathology with Dissection (thirty francs a month); Vascular Conditions of Congenital Syphilis; Observing the Carotid Ligature; Lessons on the Medullary Complications of Gonorrhea; Studies in Forensic Medicine (morgue); and Student Practice in Childbirth at Baudelocque. How was it possible for anyone to take all this in?

The students had already begun to scatter toward their classrooms when Fernand finally found his name and assigned class: Professor Henri Thoinot's course on forensic medicine. Amazed, Fernand learned that he was going to begin learning how to care for the living by studying the dead. He followed the flow of students in the direction of the main lecture hall. At its entrance was a sculpture representing Theory and Practice reaching out toward each other, and indeed the entire hall was conceived as a shrine to the virtues of the Hippocratic science. There were paintings representing bloodletting and delivery; large frescoes depicting scenes from the history of pharmacy, osteology, and botany; medallions garlanded with oak leaves representing great doctors and surgeons. Everything was designed to inspire in students both respect of and submission to the medical world. A nearly religious silence greeted the appearance of Professor Thoinot, a wizened little man who launched immediately into his speech.

"Gentlemen, none of us has any time to lose. I will not bore you with my titles and credentials, except to provide you with this simple statistic: between 1884 and 1906, when I served as head medical examiner at the police prefecture, I performed more than five hundred forensic autopsies.

"This daily commerce with death gave me a knowledge that I hope to pass on to you. Sooner or later, every doctor must look into death, since within the cadaver are concentrated all the mysteries of human nature. That is correct, gentlemen. Only by studying the decomposition of the human body will you discover the spirit that animates its cavities, arteries, and internal organs. Believe me, a corpse is a lot more instructive—and reliable—than a conscious man.

"We will therefore divide our study into three major parts. We will begin the year by describing death by firearms, relying on last year's body count: one hundred eighteen cadavers killed by firearms and dissected at the Paris morgue. Then we will look into that area whose groundwork was so magnificently prepared by my late friend Brouardel: death by strangulation, drowning, and hanging. These are classic cases. Finally, by spring, we will have moved toward death by poisoning, a domain in which our knowledge is constantly being refreshed by the discovery of new toxins. Through forensic medicine, you will touch on all the sciences: anatomy, physics, and even chemistry. Imagine this: bloodstains can sometimes be recovered as far away as ten feet from a body. Whose blood is it? Imagine the technological advances—chemical and microscopic procedures, for example— needed to give Cain his just desserts, to distinguish with certainty the victim's blood from that of the accused.

"Forensic medicine is not merely a science of the body but of the mind. And here we come to one of its most interesting aspects: telling a real murderer from an unintentional one. Does he carry the marks of cruelty on his face? We will return later to such questions, which touch upon metaphysics, and will begin, if you don't mind, with firearm wounds."

Fernand hung on each one of Professor Thoinot's words. After an interesting disquisition on the removal of corpses to mortuaries came the examination of the cadaver and study of the clothing, during which, Thoinot reminded them, every detail had to be considered, from tiny tears to burn "tattoos." This occasioned a highly elaborate classification of bullet wounds, from the fissure wound to the cul-de-sac wound, since the same bullet could go through several segments of the body or, inversely, several gunshots could look as if they came from a single source. To shed light on these mysteries, one had to scrutinize the entry and exit points of the bullets, starting with the principle that entry wounds were smaller than exit wounds and that the former would have an encrustation of powder stains around their perimeter.

Next came the delicate question of dating the gunshot wound. Ante- or postmortem? Here again smoke deposits and encrusted powder grains would illuminate matters. Fernand followed with fascination the multiple hypotheses, absorbed by this human chess game. At the very pinnacle of suspense, Professor Thoinot ended his lecture, closed his ring binder, and told the students he would see them again the following week.

The hall remained silent after his departure. It had been a masterful performance. If the other professors were that entertaining, it would be a good year. Returning students passed the word along that the other lecturers would be far less interesting.

Several minutes later, a stylish-looking man stepped up to the platform. His hair was dyed and he wore a tight dark corduroy suit, his torso covered in a multicolored vest. Leaning on a gold-handled cane, he greeted the students in a small, thin voice. Here was Daniel Andréotti, the renowned dermatologist from the Hospital Saint-Louis, a pretentious dandy whose chief obsession was skin anomalies: psoriasis, purpuras, and other annoyances. As he mentally picked at the blotches, pimples, and eruptions that had attacked his patients' bodies, classifying them by category, tongues began to wag and the dull roar of bored voices to rise at the back of the lecture hall. Such interruptions seemed not to bother Professor Andréotti, who imperturbably continued his lecture.

Fernand used the occasion to take out his snack. This museum of horrors had given him an appetite. He munched on the piece of *saveloy*—a kind of sausage—he had carefully hidden inside a pocket of his schoolbag.

Behind him, the older students were busy assembling a list of the best professors. On it were such names as Adolphe Pinard, director of obstetrics at Baudelocque Hospital; Samuel Pozzi, chief of gynecology at Broca Hospital; the legendary Raphaël Blanchard, who was the founder of the colonial Institut de Médecine and a specialist in medical numismatics; and the celebrated Jules Déjérine, grand master of neurology at Saltpêtrière Hospital. Lamaze had of course not yet chosen his specialty, though secretly he was drawn to the mysteries of the brain, the study of which he had begun by taking several courses with Hippolyte Bernheim back in Nancy.

By this point the noise in the lecture hall was nearly deafening. One could barely hear Professor Andréotti discuss—which he did, in passionately lyrical tones—rampant cases of hair loss due to tenacious dermatoses, a particularly lucrative disease for doctors in his field. As he spoke, some wags were quietly passing around a satirical pamphlet that made fun of Andréotti, entitled "Save Your Skin from Your Doctor." At the time of its release, this small bible for iconoclasts had been a runaway best-seller, and delighted students scrambled to buy whatever copies they could find. The book lambasted everything that was wrong in the world of medicine—but focused in particular on doctors whose patients had the highest mortality rates, as well as those who scoffed at following sterile procedures; these latter would drop their instruments on the floor while they were operating, calmly pick them up, and continue to operate. According to the authors of the pamphlet, medicine had made great strides in spite of doctors, who were notoriously incompetent and arrogant petty tyrants.

Andréotti might have been on the list of hopeless incompetents, but he seemed unaware of the restlessness of his audience and monotonously pursued his subject. That is, until a student stood up and shouted at the top of his lungs, "A boil is a subcutaneous volcano." This unexpected and witless jibe unleashed widespread guffawing throughout the lecture hall; even the most timid students joined in. At last Professor Andréotti realized the case was hopeless, closed his notebooks, and shambled off.

New students flocked into the lecture hall from every direction. Among them, Fernand noticed, were older ones, lugging schoolbags packed to bursting. The room became more rowdy. Fernand felt like an outsider, a witness to the imbecilic mob mentality—sheeplike minds turned into grotesque caricatures. He was about to leave the lecture hall when someone called out to him.

"Hey, kid, what's the matter with you? Wet your pants? Don't leave yet. Old Nicolas is about to arrive and we're going to throw him a party. Take this and stick around!"

Fernand felt something sticky oozing between his fingers. They had shoved a rotten tomato into his hand. He was about to heave it at the student's head, but a young redheaded man with a freckled face stopped him. Fernand swore at him, then worked his way toward the exit.

The lecture hall was turning into a madhouse. New students swarmed in from every direction, their arms full of rotten eggs and apples, bloody chicken heads, rancid meat, and other delicacies, filling the hall with a nauseating odor. Who was the intended victim?

A little man entered, immediately noticeable for his servile manner, and the room went silent—which Fernand found far more disquieting than the rowdy din. He was the anatomy professor, M. Nicolas, a replacement for Professor Poirier, who, as it later turned out, had been suddenly transferred to a different school. Like an animal at bay, Nicolas studied his students for a long time, as if trying to find some sign of acknowledgment of his presence. Then, without bothering to mention the absence of his esteemed predecessor, he launched into a long lecture, delivered in a monotone, about the contents of the thoracic and abdominal cavities. The silence he was met with seemed to embolden Nicolas. His tone got more pedantic and doctoral, revealing that at heart he was an insufferable bore.

Suddenly there was a loud battle cry, which rang in Fernand's ears for a long time. A hailstorm of food was launched at Nicolas, spattering his suit with impressive precision. The hounds were loose and attacking their quarry. Blood from the chickens splattered everywhere. Things degenerated further when in a mad fury the students started fighting among themselves. When they wouldn't stop, the police were summoned to restore order. Fernand had just enough time to notice that the portrait of Martin Akakia, Francis I's physician, had been defaced, before someone hit him on the head with a stick and he collapsed unconscious on the floor.

Edgar Larquin

WHEN FERNAND REGAINED CONSCIOUSNESS, a burning pain wracked his skull; he had difficulty opening his eyes, which were glued together by coagulated blood.

"Those bastards really banged you up!"

Fernand couldn't see who was speaking to him. His lacerated forehead was still bleeding. Finally he managed to pry open his eyelids and look at whomever it was who was talking to him. He saw the red-haired student he had met in the lecture hall; the young man was staring at him while sipping a large pastis behind the counter of a café.

"Whatever you do, don't move. You'll lose more blood. Alfred's going to bring you some warm wine. It'll do your arteries good."

Even in his pain and confusion, Fernand wondered how anybody who studied medicine could believe in something so silly. But the pain was so intense that he swallowed his anger and lay back down on the dirty green bench covered in worn moleskin—he realized he was in Alfred Lebon's Café des Poitevins, located across from the School of Medicine. This seedy hovel was a meeting place for Left Bank intellectuals and medical students from the various hospitals—Salpêtrière,

Charité, Necker, Enfants-Malades, Laënnec, Cochin—who valued it for its dancers, phony Spanishness, and exiles from the Place Maubert (dubbed "the Maube"). Everybody in this little bohemia got along well; it was a popular trading post for hospital gossip and racetrack tips.

"Those bastards thought we were going to welcome old Nicolas with open arms! As if we would forget all about the great Faraboeuf—who taught there for twenty years—and let ourselves get taken in by some mumbling bore of an anatomy professor who isn't even a surgeon.

"That paper Nicolas wrote on anatomy is nothing but gibberish, a mindless catalog of muscular and tendinous fibers. The only thing it's good for is lighting fires."

Fernand listened numbly while the student held forth about the anatomy faculty, all of them authors of competing anatomy textbooks, each of which, according to the redhead, was more narrow-minded and biased than the one before.

Fernand only caught snatches of what the student—inspired by having consumed four pastis in a row—was spewing, but he did learn that the medical school's administration had been tactless enough to fire Dr. Poirier, who was the spiritual son of the famous anatomist Faraboeuf and deeply admired by his students. Poirier had been replaced by an obscure professor from Nancy, the school having decreed that there was no one in Paris worthy of the post.

Finally the student introduced himself. His name was Edgar Larquin, and he was something of a character at the medical school. His collection of poems about boils and enemas was a favorite among the regulars at M. Alfred's, where he seemed to hold court. Larquin was also a pimp, able to find available young women for inexperienced students from the country, and he had access to a boat on the Seine that was ideal for rendezvous. Larquin had also started a service for lazy students who were willing to pay handsomely for exam answers—and his discretion. However, Larquin's main source of income was from trafficking in cadavers, which he delivered for huge sums to passionate dissectors and other scalpel-wielding eccentrics whose appetites were unappeased by the stingy daily rations apportioned by the city morgue.

These diverse activities permitted him to maintain a tony bachelor flat on rue de Rohan, near Notre-Dame cathedral and the garden of Théodore de Banville. Every evening, in this Louis XII-era building (where, it was said, the ghost of Cardinal de Rohan still roamed), he entertained the seamy underside of the Paris medical establishment: students waiting to take their medical boards over again, dismissed professors, campus radicals. They drank and partied until early morning. Then Larquin would have to refill his coffers by ripping somebody else off.

A lanky, raw-boned young man burst into the café, slamming the door. Hanging from his arms were young women with spacey, titillated expressions.

"We got them!" he shouted to nobody in particular. "The school's closed down, and Dean Debove is getting kicked out. Alfred, a round for everybody!"

"Cocky, isn't he, this Louis Devraigne?" said Edgar to Lamaze with a touch of envy. "A good student and a great ladies' man. I don't care how much they say he looks like he's got head lice. He's the best fourth-year clinician I know of, and one day soon he'll be the top obstetrician."

"You know, Fernand," Larquin continued conspiratorially, "you can party more than anybody else in school and still stay at the top of the class. You just have to know how to do it. Now whatever you do, don't move. Just lie there and listen to me carefully. The great Edgar Larquin is going to complete your education tonight."

Groggy from the wine and his head wound, Fernand couldn't have summoned the strength to move his big toe. He had no choice but to listen to Larquin mouth off.

"Unless you want to end up with a pitiful salary, someone whose greatest thrill is to afford a theater matinee and whose greatest expense is a life subscription to a medical journal, don't ever forget this simple rule: Doctors need sick people. A good doctor learns to cultivate the sick the way a gardener does his roses. Your studies won't help you do that. So don't burden yourself with useless knowledge. The less you know, the more persuasive you'll seem.

"I myself have never put my nose in a textbook. Once a week the school hospital raises a flag, signaling that a woman has gone into labor, and I peek through the gate to the delivery room if I happen to be in the neighborhood. The rest of the time I relax. Sometimes I attend Samuel Pozzi's course on theory and palpate a patient the way you're supposed to, but I know that's not the way to make a career. What counts isn't knowledge but know-how and contacts.

"More than anything, a good doctor has to make a deep impression on his patient, has to make himself absolutely necessary to him. He does this through clever manipulation of obscure terminology and by at all costs never offering a clear or definitive diagnosis. That leaves every possible way open for flattering the patient's vanity. Prescribe some useless medicine, ointments, and lozenges, if that's what he likes. When his urine's cloudy, tell him it's obviously due to an obstruction of the liver. And finally, stay at his bedside even when he's cured. He'll be grateful to you for it. And don't forget this: the slower the treatments, the more profitable they'll be. Now, if you succeed after many visits in persuading your patient that his illness is unique and that thanks to you he's come through it, you've made your reputation and you can start thinking about setting up your practice in a fashionable neighborhood.

"But that's not all. You've got to do more than practice medicine. You've got to apply what I call 'political science.' You've got to be aggressive, rub shoulders with the great, read the signs of the times—becoming a nationalist or a pacifist depending on which way the wind is blowing, until you've got a client with all the right social and financial advantages. Then his fate's sealed—he'll be married body and soul to the values of his master. Every form of flattery must be employed to reach this goal. Look at Alexandre Couvelaire, predestined by his first name to conquer the world of obstetrics.

"He's an average student who took courses, along with a lot of others, with Pierre Delbet, Pierre Marie, and Champetier de Ribes. In other words, he took the classic route. Through incredible luck he ended up working with Professor Pinard at Baudelocque, that temple of Venus Callipyge and Venus Genitrix. The question I ask myself is, Was this really pure luck or the result of his machinations? Suddenly the doors to glory opened up to him. He becomes director of the hospital in 1901, director of the laboratory in 1903; he gets both his teaching license and obstetrician's license at the same time and, while waiting for his professorship, starts making plans to fill the shoes of his supervisor and father-in-law, Pinard. That's right. Wipe that look of astonishment off your face! He was smart enough to marry the boss's daughter. While the rest of us were struggling through hell in backbreaking and fruitless work, Alexandre the great was enjoying the lion's share—and getting laid. Poor Pinard! The great obstetrician is going to be replaced by a vulgar stud! It's enough to make you weep."

Larquin picked up a big red-checked napkin and pretended to blow his nose. Then he continued with his speech, after briefly gauging his listener's alertness.

"Fernand, old man, never forget how important women are to building a career. Let me give you but one example: Pozzi, my adviser, the gynecology department chair at Broca. Would you even know his name if all the female patients in Europe he'd taken care of and made love to hadn't lionized him and sung his praises? He's as sharp-looking as those brilliant pincers he invented—the ones long and slender enough to take hold of the uterus without damaging it. But this charmer owes most of his fame to the ladies to whom he's dedicated himself. He spends his days at their bedside, paying homage to their bleeding fibroids and postpartum complaints. But at night, he's on the fly with some perfumed creature, catching a boat or train to some exotic location. He's a specialist on tapeworms, and reputed to have seduced a thousand women. Gossip has it that even Judith Gautier, Louise Ackermann, and Sara Bernhardt were among them. But truth isn't the point here. What counts is persuading your patients that it's true, so that they'll want to join that spectacular hit parade. Women are still the best investment for any young doctor without a fortune. Choose the clever ones. Make them fall madly in love with you. It won't cost you a penny, and they'll make your career."

There was a bitter taste in Fernand's mouth, whether caused by the vermouth and curaçao Alfred had made him drink between two glasses of wine or by the cynicism of the advice he was being fed. Too exhausted to argue, he wanted only to get back to the institute, so that he could sleep quietly near those who were blessedly unable to speak. As he was about to leave, he was astonished to see Lison, the young maid from the institute he had seen that morning, sitting a few feet away. She was wearing a provocatively low-cut black silk dress.

"Well, well, this gentlemen obviously keeps fine company," said Edgar, who noticed Fernand nod at the young girl. "I admit that she's pretty, and probably good in bed, but if you're looking for a dose of the syph, you've hit the bull's-eye with her."

That did it. Fernand got up, prepared to fight for the honor of a girl he did not even know.

"Not only violent, but jealous! Have you got a lot to learn! Meet me at old Charbois's place, rue Mouffetard in an hour. I'll buy you some *tripe à la mode de Caen* and omelets with kidneys. That'll set you straight," shouted Edgar, running away.

The following article about the incident at the medical school appeared in the *Tribune medicale* on November 19, 1910:

On November 8, students at the medical school greeted Professor Nicolas with a volley of tomatoes, a chorus of boos, and the sound of a hunting horn. As a result, the administration has decreed that courses shall be suspended and the library closed. University officials met on Monday November 18th, at the Sorbonne, to determine what action ought to be taken as a result of these disturbances.

The doors of the medical school were still closed at the beginning of December; though Dean Debove had been dismissed from his position, his replacement had still not been named. Despite all the disruption, however, students somehow managed to keep up with their course work by forming study groups. And the individual responsible for forming the organizing body of these study groups, the Cooperative Association of Medical Students, was none other than Edgar Larquin. Larquin had managed to enlist the fifth-year students as teachers. Things went smoothly—and were even netting him a substantial profit.

Fernand decided to make the best of the situation; an extraordinary state of affairs called for extraordinary behavior. So he put away his prejudices and good-naturedly accepted the friendship of Edgar, who had sworn to teach young Lamaze what Paris was all about. He went out often, juggling daily visits to Les Halles—the colorful fruit and vegetable market where activity was constant and varied—with exhausting nights at the institute. He had gotten used to the grimacing children, and even managed to get a couple of hours of rest around them, leaving him feeling ready for more the next morning.

After several changes in location, the Cooperative Association of Medical Students finally headquartered its activities at Broca Hospital, where Edgar had quite a few friends. Every two days, at ten in the morning, the otherwise idle students came to meet in a big room whose air was permeated with the nauseating smell of phenol disinfectant, used to douse the beds. There they awaited the arrival of the master, Louis Dartigues, nicknamed "Loulou" by his friends. He would arrive precisely at 11:00, straight from the operating room, covered with blood but ready to share his enthusiasm for medicine with his young colleagues.

Dartigues was head of the hospital's gynecology clinic and reported to Samuel Pozzi. He looked like a military man and had an intimidating voice, but Dartigues was actually the gentlest of men. His one weakness was his inability to stop inventing bizarre surgical instruments. One of these was the hysterolabe, whose purpose, Dartigues wrote, was to "seize the uterus without scraping it, the way one uses a caressing, firm hand to palm the breast of a woman." He was also reputed to have created a bistoury with interchangeable blades; the yataghan knife, used for skin grafting; the autostatic quadrivalve vaginal speculum; and the weighted bivalve vaginat. Dartigues seemed genuinely to be in love with his work, and on days when he was in a really good mood he would invite students to witness a surgical procedure. This virtuoso with a blade would sometimes get so absorbed during these procedures that his scientific carving would give an insufficiently chloroformed patient quite a start. After such performances, which could leave some of the younger students unconscious on the floor, the custom was to go for a drink at old Dr. Lateux's laboratory.

Old Lateux was an eccentric little man and a contemporary of Pinard. He had devoted his life to anatomic studies and during his slack periods liked to perform "cadaveric experiments." In a little basement room that the administration had been kind enough to lend him, Lateux collected anything having to do with pregnancy. He was particularly fascinated by those "pieces" from women who had died of puerperal fever, especially the ones who had led a "bad life." He invited his students into this room, whose decor consisted of children's skeletons and bottles containing hydrocephalic fetuses and diseased uteruses, but few had the stomach to take him up on the invitation, and despite the fact that he was liberal with good wine, his laboratory was mostly deserted.

Old Lateux hoped that after his death the room would be turned into a museum of obstetric anatomy bearing his name. Thus, in an attempt to make the place a bit more lively, he decided to perform his autopsies there rather than in Broca's main lecture hall. There were objections from the students, but the old man won his case, and students found themselves forced to spend time in this macabre office, which was short on both light and air. Smoking a pipe to fumigate the odor of rot, old Lateux would lecture for an hour in front of a large glass case that held a hapless cadaver whose thoracic and abdominal cavities had been excavated. Despite his efforts, most students left after only a few minutes. Old Lateux would impassively finish his lecture for the few hardy survivors, Fernand being one of them.

Fernand was sensitive and very impressionable, but he prided himself on being able to stick out Lateux's lectures to the end. One might wonder whether some unconscious sense of morbidity kept Fernand focused on the mass of inanimate muscles, arteries, and nerves. Perhaps he was trying to locate the boundary between life and death, a subject he often discussed with old Lateux. How, he wondered, was it possible to define a state that couldn't be experienced when you were alive? Textbooks described death in scientific ways: cadaverous rigidity, the drop in body temperature, the absence of heartbeat, dilated pupils; but something was missing. Lots of cataleptic attacks or poisonings by curare had fooled experienced doctors and made the unfortunate victims pass for dead when the spark of life was still burning in them.

Old Lateux's laboratory made a deep impression on my grandfather. For his entire life he was afraid of being buried alive—of waking up one day in a hermetically sealed tomb. His will stipulated that he be injected with a large dose of strychnine after being pronounced dead. Perhaps out of a sense of solidarity with her husband, my grandmother shared his worries. My father didn't deviate from the family rule either and stipulated that he too be injected after death. I'll do the same for my mother, and I hope someone will think about doing it for me.

Bullier's

NOT EVEN EDGAR LARQUIN'S determined efforts could loosen Fernand up. The young man from the provinces disdained the basic courtesy of pretending to his friends that he enjoyed their company, and spent whole evenings with a gruff look on this face that bordered on boorishness. He rarely confided in anyone, and shied away from all friendly gestures; they tended to make him blush deeply. His private life resembled the floodplains of his youth—windswept and gloomy.

After some unsuccessful attempts to make Fernand unbend at nightclubs like the Bal Chinois and the Dourlans des Ternes, Edgar Larquin decided to resort to desperate measures. He therefore dragged his country charge to a famous nightclub called Bullier's, a veritable "temple of voluptuousness" located on the boulevard Port-Royal, a few steps away from the Luxembourg Gardens.

Bullier's was especially popular on Thursdays, when lowlifes and middle-class folk would mix freely. The front of the club featured a statue of a roguish woman. Inside, ladies in dresses with long trains mingled with foppish men wearing shepherd costumes; they in turn mingled with hard-drinking working-class people—butlers, seamstresses from the musical theater, errand boys, and sales clerks. Everyone made for the famous Moroccan tent, which pulsated with the frenetic rhythms of the cakewalk, the one-step, or the *matchiche,* a Brazilian dance. "That amorous, metaphysical dance with one's servants," Fernand had once read in a newspaper article about the club. The whole concept of it shocked him, but he could understand the appeal. Inside the Moorish rooms, decorated with blue and red arabesques, the atmosphere was circuslike. Someone was dressed as a sewer grill. Another was doing double-jointed gymnastics. A third was doing a version of La Goulue, dancing with youths whose faces were masked by shiny cotton dominoes. A group of students were chatting among African statues on cast-iron ottomans, surrounded by stucco columns.

It had been Edgar's bright idea to come disguised as a surgeon. He pranced around in his surgeon's cap, a pair of butcher's scissors hanging from his waist, accompanied by a back-alley abortionist, a eunuch, and some nurses in army coats. Uncomfortable with so much exuberance, Fernand stayed by himself, in a little room where people were playing billiards. The crowd surged, the excitement mounted. A fat woman, beneath whose camisole hung pendulous breasts, climbed onto a chair and was honking like a goose. Leaning against a bust of old Bullier himself was a French soldier with a rum-colored mustache, spitting on the parquet and spewing out a string of obscenities.

Fernand found the atmosphere stifling. Toward midnight, nauseated by the heady perfumes of ylang-ylang and opopanax gone bad, mixed with acrid sweat and smoke, he went outside for some fresh air. He felt out of sync with this world. His stomach was in knots, as if deep inside he was nursing some unnamable grievance. He had rarely felt at ease—except as a child, when he went hunting for crayfish near the Moselle—but in Paris he felt more out of sorts than ever. What was he going to do with his life? Waste it, like Edgar and his cronies, by looking for a good time? He hadn't been brought up

that way: he didn't have a gift for being carefree. His youth was ending, and he'd never really had the chance to enjoy it.

The sound of fighting yanked him out of his depressed reverie.
Two rough-looking types, perhaps dockworkers, had grabbed a guy
in a gray cap who was threatening them with a knife. Their faces
were poorly lit by the paper lanterns festooning the trees, but Fernand could see that the man in the cap was wearing mismatched
gloves—one canary yellow, the other black—and had a gardenia in
his buttonhole. Not the uniform of a pimp.

Holding his breath, Fernand crept closer. The two dockworkers
had managed to get the man's hands pinned behind his back. They
were forcing him to kneel. Terrified, not knowing what he should
do, Fernand watched as the men began viciously striking the man,
who was now doubled over, sighing as each blow landed. Fernand
was on the verge of coming to his aid when a delicate, beringed hand
touched his shoulder and a melodious voice whispered in his ear:
"Don't say a word. Follow me." There was the overwhelming odor of
musky perfume.

Suddenly he was being blindfolded by a thick scarf and pulled
backward. Fernand was still thinking about the fight, and wondering
what he should do. He started to pull away, but at that moment the
cries of the man being beaten were turning into moans of pleasure.
Confused, Fernand went limp, allowing himself be led away by his
mysterious captor.

They came to a grove of trees. His captor tugged on his coat
sleeve, signaling for him to sit down. Still hidden behind him, she
gently slipped her arms around him. He could feel a thin, sinewy
body moving against him with such professional dexterity that he
found it impossible to resist. Her hands explored his body expertly,
depriving him of the small amount of will that remained. Panting
and perspiring, Fernand was moving toward the inevitable conclu-

sion of such an encounter. Though the voice behind him told him not to, Fernand couldn't resist. He tore off his blindfold and threw himself hungrily upon this creature. Rather than the nymph of his dreams, he saw, lying half-nude on the grass, the frail body of Lison. Silently he contemplated her watery eyes and pale skin. Reading his expression, Lison pulled down the tunic she'd been wearing in place of a dress and, without saying a word, disappeared into the night.

Not knowing whether to laugh or cry, Fernand sank into the grass and closed his eyes. A heavy odor of musk floated in the air. The party was coming to an end and the last revelers were about to leave, their faces looking wan and defeated in the light of dawn. The man in the gray cap staggered by, struggling to put his monocle back in place. Makeup was running down his wrinkled face, which gave the impression of an old, tired clown, grotesque and pathetic.

Bullier's was strewn with deflated balloons, greasy paper, and cigarette butts; the "palace of dreams" seemed funereal. Fernand searched in vain for his friends, but Edgar Larquin and company had already left for more intense, more dangerous pleasures than those on the boulevard Port-Royal.

Rather than return to the institute, Fernand decided to brave the cold of this raw December morning. He made his way toward the banks of the Seine. On the way, he passed a carnival that was setting up its tents and a small zoo. Shivering acrobats under frost-encrusted canvas sheets greeted him and told him to come back at noon for the freak show. Paris was deserted, almost unrecognizable under its thin white shroud. Lamaze fought the gusts of wind. He was still haunted by the milky whiteness of Lison's body. What was it about her that attracted him so desperately?

At the top of the Saint-Michel Bridge, Fernand stopped. Chunks of ice flowed along the Seine. The young man determined to get Lison in bed.

Lison

LISON HAD LEFT HER hometown in Normandy in the spring of 1907 and come to Paris. She had had enough of country life and milking cows and dreamed of building a career as an actress, like Sarah Bernhardt. In the capital she would find her rich benefactor. She soon enough learned the truth. On the boulevard Sebastopol she met a fat man with a ring who told her he was a stage manager for a theater company. He took her to a café for a drink and there promised her a role in the next production. Before Lison had even learned her lines, however, she was forced to leave the stylish apartment in which the fat gentleman had settled her.

There followed a quick decline in lifestyle and living situations: furnished hotels in the Latin Quarter, then furnished rooms on the boulevards, and finally an unheated attic room without running water on the sixth floor of a dilapidated building in the Maube. Lison decided to try to get her life back on track and, on the advice of a fellow fallen woman, went to a placement agency for domestic workers. But when she saw the bitter look and dry hands of the woman who ran the place, she decided to try to make it on her own and went back to haunting the public toilets, going from one opportunity to the next—a path that led her to Saint-Lazare Prison.

Located in the suburb of Saint-Denis, Saint-Lazare was run by the sisters of Marie-Josèphe Convent and actually enjoyed a fairly good reputation. It was a place where prostitutes could get a clean room and a square meal before going back to the abuse of their handlers. The sisters introduced the women to the mysteries of sewing and the Bible, giving them a veneer of respectability that, if they used it wisely, could sometimes attract a better class of clientele.

Here Lison met the man who would be her benefactor—Father Stéphane, a confessor of lost souls who roamed the hallways of the prison in his big black cassock. Everything about him suggested how seriously he took his mission of saving souls. Every morning he arrived, rosary in hand, to fight evil.

Lison fell under his sway almost immediately. Having failed miserably in her theatrical ambitions, the life of the cloister began to attract her. Father Stéphane sensed that he had won a convert, got her an early release, and found her a job working as a maid at the Institute of the Deaf and Dumb, where he served as director. This served two purposes: to give her productive work and keep her close to him. At the institute Lison was quickly brought down to earth as far as Father Stéphane's intentions went, and soon was paying dearly for her mystical passions. A hardworking maid by day, she had to share the saintly man's cot at night—and all for a miserable salary.

Nonetheless, she also learned that the priest wasn't altogether a bad man. As she got more used to things, she even found herself moved by his mix of hardness and tenderness. Sobbing, he described the day that God had deserted him. Tired of giving communion and saying a rosary he no longer believed in, he had turned to vice with the enthusiasm of a novice. Lison was his enlightened guide through the world of lust, feeding him flesh and protecting him from prying looks. In return he gave her the occasional evening off, during which she took her turn hunting for rare, unusual pleasures. Vice can be dangerous. As Lison slipped down that steep, torturous path of desire, her body rebelled at all the degradation by giving up on her. With a kind of detachment, she let herself decay, having decided that what was coming was the inevitable culmination of her wasted life.

In the pale morning light, everything became clear. The costume balls at Bullier's were over for Lison. She struggled up the six flights of stairs, stopping to catch her breath on each landing.

The door creaked as she opened it. Her future seemed as narrow as this cubbyhole she called a room. A large mirror hung over her ramshackle iron bed. She tried to avoid her reflection, but something forced her to look. She had become another woman: gray, thin, with spindly legs. Her chest and thighs were covered in blisters. Under the white skin of her neck, a painful gland had erupted. There was nothing more she could do. In a rage, she threw the calomel ointment prescribed for her by a doctor. They were all quacks and charlatans. During a very expensive visit to a highly respected doctor, she had been told that a daily diet of carrots and raw turnips would slow the progress of the disease. Now she knew the truth—the confirmation of what she had suspected when the first symptoms appeared.

She had always been healthy, vital, and strong; never a sick day in her life. Now she felt weak, listless. Her vision had become blurred; there were burning flashes of pain in her head. She had awakened one morning and realized that she could remember nothing. She had tried to get up, but her legs gave out, and she was found sprawled unconscious on the floor. That's when they quietly began saying things like "primary lymph stage" and "gummatous rashes." But Lison understood perfectly what was happening to her; the damage was done, and there was nothing she could do about it.

She went to bed in her clothes after drinking a large dose of chloral hydrate. Soon the medicine began to work, soothing her suffering. Fernand's face appeared one more time, in a mist, before disappearing completely.

Fernand learned about Lison's death the next morning. Her concierge said that she had died in horrible pain. A man of the cloth, somebody who often visited her, had been sobbing at her bedside all night. According to the doctor who was there at the end that night, she had gone into a crisis known as childbirth syndrome, a rare condition that appears among those suffering from tertiary syphilis. The victim experiences flashes of pain that feel like labor—caused by the excruciating impression that a head is passing through the pelvis, which causes violent contractions and contortions in the body—until suddenly they simply cease, as if the baby has been born. At that very moment, Lison's heart had stopped.

That same evening, Fernand handed Father Stéphane his resignation and left the Institute for the Deaf and Dumb. He felt more pity than hate for the priest, who would now know peace; he pretended that he suspected nothing. From that day forward, he stopped frequenting Edgar and his crew, and got rid of everything that reminded him of Lison. That chapter of his youth was over.

PART TWO

THE CROSSROADS

Our fates and our wishes play
out almost in counterpoint.
　　　　　　　—VICTOR HUGO

Family Secrets

WHO WAS THE REAL "good Dr. Lamaze"? The more I read and reread his notes, notebooks, and diaries, the less the pieces of the puzzle of his personality seemed to fit together. I couldn't quite grasp what lay behind the smiling face of the plump man enshrined on my mother's dressing table.

How could a man devote himself to liberating women from suffering that was sanctioned by the Bible—and by so doing stand up to God, the Church, and the entire medical world—and at the same time make crude misogynist jokes? Did this man who had a "taste for women"—as he wrote—really love them? Was his career really guided by the sense of devotion and "deep humanism" that others saw in him?

When I visited my mother at the hospital, I cautiously tried to bring up the subject of her father, but the conversations went nowhere. Instead of talking about him as a father or a man, she always saw him as a doctor. If anything, however, she maintained a certain reserve toward the memory of her father, as if she wanted to save all her affection for her mother, Louise.

Lamaze remained hidden to me. This fired my determination to make my research into his life more systematic. Those who were around during the heyday of the Lamaze Method were growing scarce. I drew up a meager list of the few surviving family members.

Being an only child never bothered me. My father, who had been born in 1900 and was twenty-five years older than my mother, Anne-Marie, became a great-grandfather of children from a first marriage before I had even finished school. I didn't know much about my half-sisters and half-brother; they were roughly the same age as my mother. I used to astound my classmates when I told them that by the age of seventeen I had already become the great-aunt to four children.

Apart from that unusual chronology, the Gutmann family history was a total mystery to me, a mystery maintained by silence whenever I tried to broach the subject. Nonetheless, bits and pieces reached me in indirect ways, such as when I found out that Fernand Lamaze had been a tutor to my father, whose name was Jean. I also learned that my father had stuttered as a child. And that Jean's stepfather, Emile Gutmann, had been a longtime friend of Fernand's. In the garden of Emile's *hôtel particulier* on avenue Denfert-Rochereau, my mother had played with the children of the man who would eventually become her husband.

It was when I happened to be reading the correspondence between Marc Bloch and Lucien Febvre—two of the most famous French historians of the twentieth century and founders of the scholarly review *Annales d'histoire sociale et économique*—that I learned more about the relationship between Fernand Lamaze and Emile Gutmann. In their letters the names of Lamaze and Gutmann were associated: "Do you know that *Annales* owes two of our first five subscribers to me? It was our good friend Emile Gutmann who brought us Dr. Lamaze," writes Bloch to Febvre in 1928, proud that a banker and a young doctor have subscribed to this review since its first issue.

Gutmann and Lamaze had much in common: an insatiable curiosity and a distrust of cliques, closed societies, and any form of intellectual prison. Their friendship lasted nearly thirty years, ending on May 19, 1940—a month before the Germans marched into Paris—which was both Emile's birthday and the day he chose to kill himself in his garden. A few weeks earlier he had asked Fernand about how best to commit suicide with a gun. Knowing that lying to such a perceptive man was futile, Fernand had shown him the location of the vein leading to the heart. He had begged Emile to flee France, but his friend wouldn't listen. His family would leave, but he would stay. He had been awarded the Croix de Guerre, was a chevalier of the Legion of Honor, and above all he was a Frenchman of "Israelite origins" who had passed the age of running away; his hope was to rest in peace in the country he called home.

The afternoon Emile died, Fernand was called to his bedside. He closed his friend's eyes, as he had promised he would do. He remembered the first time they had met. It was in 1913, in Emile's office. Emile had hired Fernand to tutor his son Jean, on the advice of an eccentric American friend. At the time, Fernand was twenty-two years old and struggling to finish medical school. After his depressing experience at the Institute for the Deaf and Dumb, Fernand had been surviving on the meager allowance his father sent him and on what he earned working as a waiter at a dive in the Maube and as an undertaker at the Roblot Company. He was leading the kind of life typical for a medical student at the time and had cut out all luxuries—except drinking absinthe and visits to the brothel, two habits he believed essential to his physical and mental well-being.

At the time he met Emile, Fernand was at a crossroads. Though fascinated by the workings of the body, he also felt genuine empathy for the sick. He attracted the attention of two professors, Louis Dubrisay, a renowned obstetrician, who was hoping Lamaze might succeed him in his position, and Gustave Roussy, who was pushing Fernand toward a career in neurology, which was both the most lucrative field of medicine and the one that demanded the most patience and money. When Prosper got wind of his son's bad habits, he cut off his living expenses, and Fernand was suddenly and keenly aware of the gulf separating those with money from those without. What he needed was a job that wouldn't take up too much of his study time and yet also help him survive in the Parisian jungle. Rent was due, the cupboard was empty, and Fernand was wearing himself out with his nighttime escapades. Things got so bad that he was considering going back to the Lorraine, when he came across an ad in a medical gazette that would turn his life around. "LADY LIVING ALONE WITH SERIOUS EYE PROBLEMS OFFERS POSSIBLE LODGING IN SAINT-GERMAIN TO CULTIVATED YOUNG GIRL WHO CAN READ TO HER EACH EVENING" read the ad. Fernand didn't waste a minute; he knew he was the man for the job. He mingled with a crowd of prim-looking governesses outside Bettina Del Rio's *hôtel particulier*.

Though eighty, Betty Paxton (her maiden name) was still irresistibly charming, and had determined to enjoy her last years by frittering away what remained of her enormous fortune on her fantastic whims. Some years earlier she had started pretending to be suffering from a disabling eye disease, which gave her the excuse to hire a female companion. This time she had interviewed half a dozen old maids, each one more boring and musty than the one before, when a bearded young man with a sensitive, intelligent face swept into the room. She didn't hesitate; she offered him room and board in exchange for five evenings of readings a week.

Fernand was blessed with a prodigious memory. He had memorized an enormous amount of French poetry and could recite whole passages from novels by Balzac and Flaubert (particularly *Salambô*, Flaubert's historical novel about Carthage, a copy of which he kept on his bedside table). Taking his new job to heart, he decided to roll up his sleeves and introduce his student, who was originally from the American West, to the finer pleasures of Voltaire's language. He was quickly disappointed. She found Voltaire "old-fashioned," Balzac "too complicated," and Stendhal "boring." She yawned as he read classics such as *Lamentations* and fell asleep during *The Death of the Wolf.* Her case seemed hopeless. Fearing for his job, Fernand decided to stick to reading the insipid prose of the stories serialized in *Le Figaro.*

Their readings would take place each evening at eight in Betty's boudoir. Wearing an orange silk tunic, curled up among her cats on a couch covered with cushions made from an American flag, she closed her eyes and listened with a delighted, hungry smile to the endless stories of lovers and disappointed husbands. However, the most flamboyant melodrama seemed drab next to the story of Betty's own life. Fernand very quickly gave up the job of reader to assume that of confidant. He learned that at the tender age of fifteen Betty had run away from a ranch in Texas to join up with a rich Brazilian shipowner. Upon the fortuitous death of this husband, she decided to begin life as a free spirit by scaling the peaks of the Himalayas, but soon discovered she was not really cut out for the ascetic life. So she traded the pristine air of Tibet for the tainted splendor of Europe. After several years of living in sumptuous Venetian palaces, she left for Paris, where she became scandalously well known for her tart tongue and audacious manners. More than one great man's fortune gave up the ghost in her arms. As old age began to approach, she settled down and married a prosperous man with a plant nursery near Paris. He entertained her with stories of the secret loves of Bengali roses. To her astonishment, she fell into the trap studiously avoided by all good courtesans and ended up falling in love with him, then following his mortal remains to the cemetery in tears.

When Fernand met Betty she was extremely fat and heavily made up. Rejected by both high and low society, she punctuated her life with chance encounters, looking for other flamboyant, sensitive types to help her bear the passage of time. She knew immediately that Fernand was one after her own heart, and tried to understand his contradictions—he seemed to her both out of step with the world and yet deeply romantic, despite his medical student's bravado. How, she wondered, could someone quote long passages of poetry and yet satisfy his needs with almost clinically scheduled visits to the whorehouse? Love and arithmetic were not good bedfellows. She found in him a curious mix of shamelessness and Puritanism. There were other contradictions. His coldly scientific sensibility had mystic impulses; his placid sense of duty hid a tortured side. In short, to Betty, Fernand was endlessly surprising, and despite her advanced age and a certain knowledge of the human soul, which a woman learns only in the reclined position, she felt lucky that fate had sent her such an intriguing companion.

Their friendship lasted until January 16, 1914, when Betty's colorful life ended on her starred couch, in that cloud of incense she liked to burn in memory of past voyages. She left behind more than thirty thousand francs of debts, plus a mortgage on all her property. Her burial in Père Lachaise (final resting place of Oscar Wilde, Heloise and Abelard, and Proust, among many others) was entirely paid for by her friend and banker Emile Gutmann, to whom she entrusted her cats and the duty of watching over the career of young Fernand Lamaze.

The Gardens at Denfert-Rochereau

BEFORE SHE DIED, Betty must have sensed that her days were numbered, for she resolved to go out into the social world again; she found Fernand's presence as indispensable as a walking stick. "You've got to learn to clear your head and live free," she stubbornly repeated to him, while taking him to gala matinees at the Thé Tango or openings at the Louvre, where there was as much talk about the races as about what was happening in the world. The museum was always packed with attractive women in fashionable outfits, which Betty would analyze with surgical precision.

It was in June 1913, on one of these social occasions to which Betty dragged him, that Fernand met the woman who would become my paternal grandmother. Madeleine Gutmann-Hinstin (Einstein before it was gallicized) had come in place of her husband to a garden party given by the American ambassador to honor forty-seven Boy Scouts whom Mayor Sidney Peixotto was sending on a trip around the world. One of these promising young globetrotters was Betty's grandnephew.

While American and French Boy Scouts fraternized under brightly colored banners, Lamaze spied a woman who looked as if she had stepped out of an Impressionist painting. Draped in gauzy tulle, her face shadowed by a wide-brimmed hat, Madeleine did not in the least conform with Fernand's notion of a banker's wife, and certainly not Betty's banker. She asked Fernand about his studies and then talked to him for quite a long time about her son Jean, an amiable but nervous child with a worrisome case of stuttering that had resisted treatment by the leading specialists. Short of money and eager to humor her financier's family, Betty praised her protégé's teaching capabilities. And that is how Fernand became the tutor of his future son-in-law.

Jean was the son of Madeleine's first marriage to Maximilien Dreyfus. He had barely known his father, who died of a mysterious disease on February 9, 1902, after having been found in a coma in a London hotel. My Grandmother Madeleine was the daughter of Gustave Hinstin, to whom the Comte de Lautréamont dedicated his *Poésies*. Hinstin was a brilliant professor of rhetoric and top Hellenist and Latinist (his translations of Euripides and Virgil are still in use) whose career had been tarnished near the end by accusations of pedophilia. His death on July 3, 1894, silenced the rumors.

Widowed not long after her father's death, Madeleine decided to marry a man she had loved since childhood. Emile Gutmann was her second cousin, which kept it all in the family. However, they waited eight years to get married, and during those eight years, my father, Jean, was the only man in the lives of his grandmother (Gustave's widow) Jeanne, and Madeleine, whose attention he monopolized day and night. Emile Gutmann's arrival in the cloistered world of avenue Denfert-Rochereau traumatized the child, producing what seemed incurable stuttering as well as increasingly violent outbursts of anger. He was thirteen when Fernand met him, likeable and charming but unable to control a temper that would only get worse with age.

Fernand was only nine years older than his pupil. He dreaded that first lesson on avenue Denfert-Rochereau, arriving fifteen minutes early with sweaty palms; he was unnerved by the idea of tutoring a kid who could have been his younger brother. A maid answered the door and took him through a maze of corridors to a small office where Jean was expecting him. Convinced that his new mentor was a spy hired by his stepfather, the boy reacted with hostility to Fernand's arrival, rocking back and forth in his chair during the entire one-hour lesson without once opening his mouth to speak. When Madeleine appeared at five o'clock to invite them to tea, Fernand was talking nonstop, as if trying to make up for his charge's complete silence.

The little cakes served with scalding Darjeeling did nothing, unfortunately, to change Jean's mood, and to his mother's despair he maintained his ominous silence. By this point Fernand had also lapsed into silence, quietly observing the room, which looked more like an office than a living room. Like the rest of the apartment, it was littered with boxes. Paintings and books were piled on the floor. It was nothing like the hothouse atmosphere he had been expecting. Madeleine and Emile showed little interest in decorating, choosing to make piles of the objects they had purchased for either aesthetic or investment purposes. Emile had decided to follow the fashion for modern art and was purchasing anything he could by the Fauves, Expressionists, and other avant-garde artists.

In an attempt to liven up the conversation, Madeleine launched into a detailed description of her most recent musical and pictorial discoveries. She chatted about the Russian Ballet then performing at the Champs-Elysées, claiming that it not only revolutionized classical ballet but changed the way we view the world. Fernand, whose cultural education was limited to what he had learned in a schoolhouse in the Lorriane, an education that didn't extend much further than the Romantics and the Symbolists, listened in fascination. He was somewhat in awe of Madeleine—perhaps it was her aquamarine eyes, her flawless skin, or that indescribable perfume that saturated the air, lingering behind after she had left the room.

Jean drank in every word his mother spoke; and she never took her eyes off him. With his blue eyes and long brown lashes, he was physically a beautiful child—Madeleine's proudest creation. Fernand watched them, wondering what effect such exclusive, unconditional love would have on the boy's development. He seemed to realize he would have to free Jean from his mother's apron strings and began talking about studies that proved the positive effects fresh air had on stuttering. What was necessary, he argued, was to get the boy out of Paris. Long walks in the mountains would be just the thing.

My father never spoke much about his past, but he was marked for life by those exhausting walks he was forced to take. Fernand, who had walked all over Paris and grown up taking long hikes in the Vosge Mountains, knew that his young charge would get winded before he would and that the best weapon for wearing down this cocky little upstart was to wear him out. He therefore showed him no pity on these excursions, convinced that Jean's aching feet would force him to give in.

But I also believe that my grandfather's talent as a storyteller helped him win the battle against Jean's silence. He could make Paris came to life with legends and stories; even the stones were drenched in history. He introduced my father to the mysteries of Place Maubert, treated him to strolls through the Bièvre, and gave him elaborate descriptions of the clientele at every dive and restaurant in the city. Fernand introduced Jean to a man named Hébert, the verger of Notre-Dame cathedral, which Fernand visited every evening. On the cathedral roof, with its breathtaking view of the dome of the Invalides and the minarets of Trocadero, Jean listened to his young tutor talking with Hébert, who, like his father before him, was the ringer of the four bells on the north tower. My father began to see that he was dealing with an unusual man, and gradually began to open up, telling Fernand about his hopes and dreams while sitting under the shade of the cedar tree in the Jardin des Plantes, the tree that Monsier de Jussieu had brought back in his hat from Lebanon in 1735.

The most important thing Fernand did for my father was diminish the boy's hatred for his stepfather. Jean was a good musician, a skillful chess player, and unbeatable at geography and math, but depression had kept him from developing these talents. Pathologically jealous of Emile, he stubbornly butted his head against people, just as his mouth butted against syllables. Blessed with the common sense of the farmer, Fernand let matters follow their course. With time, Jean simply forgot to stutter. His family called it a miracle. Though Fernand underplayed his role, Emile Gutmann was eternally grateful to him.

Emile, who was forty-eight, had recently become one of the owners of Danon Bank, which he comanaged with André Wormser (a future cabinet minister under President Georges Clemenceau) and the Lazard brothers. This was the culmination of a remarkable career that had begun in Germany, where his father had sent him at fourteen to learn the profession at the federal bank. Moving quickly up the ladder, Emile became the director of Stielman Ansbacher & Co. several years later, and made a fortune in England. He was now not only the head of one of the most important financial institutions in Paris, he was also the director of a coffee factory with headquarters in Latin America. His background enabled him to understand the international market, and to anyone who would listen, including Fernand during their very first meeting, he would argue for the need for a world bank, a "bank of banks." This was, thought Emile, the ultimate solution to the problem of gold circulation.

For Fernand, getting to know this large, warmhearted, and benevolent man was like finding a second home, after months of exile in Paris. Emile had a way of making everything seem possible. As familiar with Mozart's variations as he was with the fluctuations in value of the French franc, Emile was equally capable of suddenly taking off with his dog and a well-paid professional photographer to explore some little town in the provinces. The point of these expeditions was not to seek the exotic but to expand one's point of view. He returned from these little trips with photographs that he annotated with quotes from Balzac and Renan and then conscientiously classified in red and gray files, which he never touched again. These dusty files filled entire armoires and closets in the apartment on avenue Denfert-Rochereau. No one dared to suggest they served no purpose.

Although Jean and Emile never established a good relationship, Emile and Fernand remained close from first to last. Emile felt an unswerving affection for this gruff-looking rustic with the penetrating gaze and agile hands—long, pale, and lightly veined, these hands seemed so out of place that one couldn't help staring at them. Fernand himself often wondered why nature had given them to him, particularly since it had also made him otherwise clumsy and ambivalent about his body. But he was pleased to be treated as a member of the Gutmann family, and was proud of how far he had come from the fields of Lorraine, where his cousins still labored as farmers. But his well-being was precarious, and not unlike the malaise that paralyzed France in that spring of 1913. Fernand would come home from hospital duty completely exhausted and incapable of thinking about the future, sinking into the kind of dreamless sleep that is so often prelude to the worse nightmares.

The Eye of the Storm

"TAKE GOOD CARE OF my brother! And write me!" Jeanne Le Bey Taillis shouted to Fernand from the platform of the Gare de l'Est, watching with tears in her eyes as the crowd of conscripts boarded the train to join their regiment in Nancy. His arms full of bags and supplies, Fernand had a hard time finding his place in the overheated car packed with young men, who had launched into a spirited version of the "*Marseillaise*" to express their excitement and mask their fear. The train spewed smoke and moved off, hissing angrily. It was August 1914. Forty-three years of peace were over.

Once he found his place in the train, Fernand collapsed gratefully. Images of the last weeks were whirring around in his head. His life had gone into fast-forward ever since his appointment in March to Broca Hospital, where he had begun work with Professor Pozzi in gynecology. The old order was being replaced. In hindsight, Fernand could now see the warning signs. One had been the murder, on June 13, 1914, of the surgeon Aimé Guinard. The poor man had been shot in the heart in front of Notre-Dame by a patient unsatisfied with the surgery he had undergone for an anal fistula.

"What is the world coming to," lamented Pozzi when they had returned to the hospital from Guinard's funeral, "when patients begin to react to their surgery in this manner?" Three years later, Pozzi himself would be subject to an equally fatal attack in his own living room in Neuilly. A clerk from Boulogne-sur-Mer named Maurice Machu held the surgeon responsible for a badly healed sperm-duct valve. By 1914 Pozzi was beginning to realize that the medical world—in which the professor is emperor and surrounded by a court of toadying students and infatuated patients—was changing. But until then, the tall and dashingly dressed surgeon with jet-black eyes and velvet tongue held sway. In equal parts seductive and ambitious, Pozzi knew how to keep his hands clean, even in the worst situations. After gaining a reputation for hunting tapeworms, he went after the capital's most beautiful women and was appointed to Broca in a blaze of publicity. There, in between lectures, this crony of Leconte de Lisle, Robert de Montesquieu, and Marcel Proust would glide through the crowded rooms of the sick with cheerful nonchalance, offering a winning smile to the poor wretches spending their last days in the hospital's filthy wards.

Pozzi's disconcerting imperviousness to suffering left Fernand feeling stunned. He had always entered those malodorous, poorly heated rooms with a heavy heart. The overcrowding was so bad that beds had even been made on the floor. He wondered if he, too, would become a blind bureaucrat of death. On several occasions, he had been so revolted by the inhumanity of the medical world, dominated by men who cared more about their careers than about the patients in agony a few feet away from them, that he had resolved to leave it.

One morning at 5:00 A.M., the hour when so many people leave this life, Jeanne Le Bey Taillis, his best friend's sister, knocked on his door. All she had with her was a battered overnight case and a first edition of *Autumn Leaves* by Victor Hugo. Fernand watched as the young woman made herself at home in his cubbyhole of a room.

"Where is your husband?" Fernand risked timidly.

"Forgive me, but I'm so tired" were the only words Jeanne could say before falling fast asleep, fully dressed, on the only bed in the room. Fernand installed himself in the dilapidated Louis XV chair he had inherited after Betty's death, and studied his charming intruder. She was sleeping quietly on her side, her face half hidden by a swathe of brown hair that fell in waves all the way to the small of her back. Few men would resist such beauty. However, because of some mysterious law that made all amorous contact with his friend's sister incestuous, Fernand merely watched her with the tenderness usually reserved for a child.

The incongruity of the scene never occurred to him. What was happening was supposed to happen because Jeanne had decided it would. He had always suspected that a woman of her beauty and independence would never be happy with the good-for-nothing she had married, and that one day Nancy would seem too small a place for her. And here she was—unchanged and unbowed, as arrogant and aloof as ever.

As the light of the rising sun peeped through the shutters, he thumbed through the yellowing copy of *Autumn Leaves*. Perhaps the poet himself had once actually held this numbered volume in his hands. Smiling to himself, Fernand remembered the private storehouse into which he and Jean had placed their prized possessions: old papers, pipes, tobacco pouches, shiny pebbles from Guernsey. Everything that had been part of the world of magic had been reverently stored in Prosper Lamaze's attic. In that humble abode at the edge of the village of Vincey, on beds of deep eiderdown, Fernand, Jeanne, and Jean spent precious hours. Their friendship went back to early childhood, to the time when Fernand and Jean left on a crusade against the evil spirits of the forest while Jeanne concocted potions out of rose leaves. Now, because of Jeanne's arrival, something from the past had been miraculously brought back to life. Fernand closed his eyes, feeling at peace with himself. It was at nearly that moment that Archduke Francis Ferdinand was shot and killed in Sarajevo, and a war began.

War Diaries

Saturday, August 1, 1914

Left Paris, Gare de L'Est. Arrived Nancy, 2:30 A.M. Mobilization en route.

Sunday, August 2, 1914

Arrived Vincey at 5:00 in the morning. Cannon fire.

Thursday, August 11, 1914

The day before yesterday there was a train accident at the entrance to the station at Troyes. Ten men were killed, about three times that many wounded (artillery men). This morning we saw one of these poor devils getting buried. A detachment of infantry did the honors and two gravediggers walked behind.

Got to know a young doctor. Lévy-Valensi. He's decided to become a neurologist.

Wednesday, August 19, 1914

The same endless blue sky, the stifling heat, and the same boring lack of action. When will we leave here? There is after all fighting in

Alsace, and on the border, so there must be wounded to take care of. I'm champing at the bit but nothing can stop my vow to do my duty as a true radical. Long live our Nation!

Monday, August 24, 1914

Our orders are to leave for Autreville Vosge. This leg of the journey was long and rough. At Etreval they offered us coffee. At Favières, wine. We needed it to get our legs going again since you get hellishly out of breath pushing cars uphill. After Favières, we came to a region of plateaus and loose stones. At night, I'm feeling full of myself and with one blow of my saber killed a viper crossing the road. I'll have that viper put on my coat of arms. It'll look nice.

Thursday, August 27, 1914

Just outside of the village a storm begins to break our backs. In the blink of an eye, it drenches us right through our raincoats and everybody stops gossiping. There are forty-two of us with the field hospital, including two staff sergeants and four sergeants. We're a grab bag of different, sometimes weird types, from slickers from Paris to Vosges peasants from the Hauts-Chausses with thick bodies and thick minds. This all leads to sometimes interesting clashes. It doesn't take much to set us off. From morning to night it's a concert of swearing, insults, and challenges; they sound murderous but they're not. All part of basic barracks humor. Fatigue causes flare-ups, but these skirmishes at least create a feeling of activity that fills up the long idle hours at the camp. Coffee, soup, bedtime—these are the major respites of the day, welcome oases of rest that break up the day for a soldier in the field. So the days file by, each one like the one before, like rosary beads.

Thursday, August 28, 1914

Yesterday the rain stopped a little in the afternoon. I slept, or pretended to sleep, a good part of the day, just to try and fool this annoying sense of inaction. I wandered through a small wood growing on the hills of Etreval like a rare tuft of hair on a eunuch's cheek. I dragged the day along like a ball and chain.

Sunday, August 30, 1914

Nice morning with Courtin and Valensi hunting for snails. After an hour at most hunting among the vines we had a hundred of them, adding a little variety to the boredom. There was a little gunfire spaced out and coming from far away, just to remind us that this is a war. A gorgeous sun ripped through the mist; toward noon the land will be alive with it. In the evening, after prayers, we said a De Profundis in church for the soldiers who died on the battlefield. I'd gone there to take part in vespers, out of boredom, instead of taking a snooze on the hay. The chanting during vespers wasn't very impressive, but the De Profundis hit me in the gut. Actually, the environment lent itself to it: that small, simple church with its nondescript whitewashed walls, its meager altars decorated with the usual kind of religious souvenirs. They smelled strongly of Saint-Sulpice, but dusty as they were, if you used your imagination, you could almost see them as medieval. Then there was the priest in his faded finery and tarnished gold and the kneeling or standing soldiers, all inclined forward in the same impulse of piety for those who die for their country every day. Night was falling, swallowing the church and the praying crowd. Near the end a soldier belonging to our field hospital, a peasant from the Meuse, ran out, wracked by heavy sobs.

Wednesday, September 2, 1914

Courtin, Valensi, Morouval, and I went to Zion this morning. It's about a two and a half- or three-hour walk, all told. Going up was pretty rough as the sun hit our necks, but the view from the top makes you forget all about your stiff legs. My God, what a view! At the stall selling religious trinkets, run by the newest chaplain of Zion, I bought a nice little medallion as well as the art postcards published by the region of Lorraine. On that "inspired hill," to quote Barrès, we remembered those heroes who had reinvigorated his words by openly leading the most terrifically mystical and romantic lives until the end of the century, blatantly quarreling with the Church yet closer to the Supreme Being than any dogmatic priest. From the terrace to the front tip of the hill, we heard regular bursts of gunfire, in the direction of Manonvillier, and a bit more to the left, toward Dombasle-sur-Meurthe.

Friday, September 4, 1914

Forty-fourth birthday of the Republic.

Tuesday, September 9, 1914

In the afternoon, a cyclist brings us the order: we're to be ready to leave tomorrow at 5:00 A.M. Destination: Contrexéville, where we'll set up a temporary field hospital.

Saturday, September 12, 1914

We're staying at the Hotel Continental. In the morning we went with the officers to see the hospital set up by the Red Cross in the Cosmopolitain. A poor guy with a bullet in the thorax died today. People die from it every day. They nail them into a white pine box; six men slide the box into a regulation van decorated with flags and the pathetic thing goes off to the cemetery, surrounded by an armed convoy and followed by delegations from the two field hospitals.

Tuesday, September 16, 1914

Departure. A long stopover by the side of the road where I brazenly sample the sandwiches and bottle of Chablis Madeleine Gutmann sent to me for this leg of the journey. Out of 42 men in the field hospital, we were the only 5 to do the 90 kilometers from Contrexéville to Broussey without getting into a car. Us radicals can take it!

I saw this notice on the inner door of a church: "Out of respect for the Holy Sacrament, it is absolutely forbidden to spit."

Tuesday, September 22, 1914

A never-ending rain, wind, and terrible cold. Forbidden to leave the quarters. The regimental postman took some letters to Neuchâteau. The rumor, which is more persistent than ever, is that we're leaving for Amiens. Constant gunfire from the direction of Verdun. This could be to our advantage. Maybe they've started the pitiless massacre of those brutes who just burned down the cathedral at Reims.

War Diary, Continued

Friday, September 25, 1914

Reveille at 3 A.M. We leave. Board the train at noon. I gave Massy-Palaiseau a letter for my friend Jean and another for Jeanne and her mother, Mme Le Bey Taillis, both of whom are really worried about him. A lady is supposed to mail them in Paris. In Versailles I scribble another card for Madeleine Gutmann. She must feel so alone since Emile and Jean left. One was too young and the other too old to be called up, but they had to follow their courage. It's 8 P.M. when we arrive. The embarkation at the station takes place in a volley of curses, cuffs, and the senseless punishments of those who are at the end of their rope. We spend the night at the Vautrin barracks. This is my first contact with a barracks. It doesn't thrill me. It smells of mildew, old leather, and sour urine.

Wednesday, October 7, 1914

Saint-Saveur. In the afternoon, Valensi and I went all the way to Amiens on foot. We arrived in the city plastered with dust and wandered about aimlessly, just happy for the activity in the stores and on the sidewalks that clacked under our heels. Before leaving, we went to see the cathedral, all pink under the setting sun.

Monday, October 12, 1914

This morning an Austrian plane known as a "Taube"—black point hardly perceptible in the deep blue of the sky—passed over Saint-Saveur. The rumor is that it must have gone down near Amiens. Two Taube flew over Paris yesterday and dropped 20 bombs on the city. These Lohengrins are aiming for Notre-Dame. After Reims! Good heavens! Can anyone still boast to me about civilization across the Rhine?

Sunday, October 18, 1914

It's raining. Same old crap, in our Sunday best. Narcy brought a photograph back from Amiens showing one of those sluts who spread their legs for the soldiers garrisoned there. On the other side of the picture, the pretentious little thing has written in a painful scrawl, "Souvenir of the encampment of the Twentieth Corps."

Tuesday, October 20, 1914

Woken up suddenly. We're going to Picquigny, a little town eight kilometers from Saint-Sauveur. Our mess hall is in a vacated castle, a big, cheerful red-brick building where the cold stings as it does in the countryside. In the nave of the chapel is a copy of Rubens' *Descent from the Cross* (Lille Museum) that is gorgeous. The sacristy has some vestments embroidered by Madame de Sévigné, a good friend of the Duc de Chaulnes, Lord of Picquigny. In the choir are two reliquaries, one from the eleventh century and the other from the seventeenth. On the left, as you enter, cut into the wall at an angle, is a Saint Antoine, sculpted right into the wood by some innocent and pious hand. The little statue was so incredibly exciting that I thought about it all day and all night.

Monday, November 9, 1914

If we really are going to Amiens, to the hospital for contagious diseases, I want to be assigned to a combat troop. Great thanks to the profession of emptying chamber pots and rinsing spittoons. But there are enough chickens who'll be happy to do that. I want to fight, fight!

Tuesday, November10, 1914

Three hours to get to Amiens. Nihil mirari! [Latin: "nothing to see"] The hospital is on rue Lavaland, in an old Jesuit monastery that's been empty since the separation of church and state. We've barely moved in and we already have 102 patients, the poor wretches worn out with fever and fatigue. A lot of typhus cases, pneumonia, pleurisies, the complete opposite of being behind the scenes in the trenches.

Monday, November 16, 1914

What a dog's life! Ran all over the city to visit the sick. . . . It wouldn't be so bad if you didn't constantly run up against bureaucratic indifference and administrative incompetence all the time. They won't give us sheets, beds, medicine. Must we watch our soldiers in agony, powerless to help?

Tuesday, November 17, 1914

It was Gour who woke me up this morning, hugging me. I couldn't believe it. Little Gour, all icy from spending the night on the railroad! How a surprise like that can warm the heart and soul! It's snowing.

Saturday, November 28, 1914

I discovered a reading room in the *passage au Commerce*. A godsend for our lengthy stay at Amiens! Then I started to feel disappointed. It's part of a Church institution—the walls are lined with books all covered in the same pink, smelling like the sacristy and randy virgins. I'm reading about the customs of religious families. . . . The librarian is a piece of work, too, in flesh and in word. Picture her all dressed in black, a large mass of flabby, whitish skin, cone-shaped like a suppository. And from the monster's mouth the most dogmatic and stupid opinions about literature and art shoot out like rockets. This lady thinks Baudelaire is immoral!

Monday, November 30, 1914

All we've really got is a rehash of old news for lack of real news (the official press releases are so empty!). I read about the battle of the Marne and the battle of Ourcq. A narrow escape. Long live France! In the evening a pile of letters: 8! A card and a letter from Vincey, after a month with no news, a fat letter from Mme Gutmann and her son Jean, a card from Lucien Descaves, a letter from my pal the Bigot, and two money orders.

Sunday, December 6, 1914

Saint-Nicolas. Aching cold again, a strong glacial wind. Those poor devils in the trenches. I hope I can be with them before long.

Friday, December 11, 1914

Letter from Gour. It's raining, a depressing rain as I go with the chief medical officer to the evacuation hospital, the station, and then the library of the School of Medicine where a doddering librarian welcomes us to his empty bookshelves.

Thursday, December 24, 1914

The streets of Amiens are packed with motorists coming from the front who are leaving tonight, for the front lines, stuffed to bursting with rations for Christmas Eve.

Friday, December 25, 1914

Yesterday evening, we tried to celebrate Christmas Eve. Valensi, Bellet, and I went looking for the traditional foods in the city: boudin, duck pâté, bûche de Noël; but our hearts weren't in it. After dinner, we couldn't accept the depressing idea of just going to bed on such a night. In the morning, Bellet, Narcy, Massin, and I take a boat and row on the Somme and in the bogs until we can't get our breath.

Thursday, December 31, 1914

No news of Jean. I don't dare admit my worst fears. Weather still gray, rainy, with sudden gusts of wind that shake the chimneys and make the windows shake endlessly. The forest in Rozelieures, walks on the banks of the Moselle, running in the fields. . . . What's happened to my Lorraine? As night falls I remember that tall, black-haired girl in a red blouse. She washed mugs at the Deux Magots brasserie. I was in love with her. Every evening and morning, coming back from school, I took a detour to catch a glimpse of her in her kitchen, her bare arms in a zinc vat with mugs swimming in soapy water. One June evening, her sentimental and faithful knight, I climbed the gate under the window of my lady, balanced precariously on the ledge of her window. A nearby door opened suddenly. I jumped, but in my hurry to get out of there, I fell flat on my face. I let out a yell and lost consciousness. When I came to, I was in the kitchen of the brasserie, on the knees of my beloved. She was wiping the shining tears from my cheeks and rocking me in the hollow of her lap. And I, feeling pathetic, drowning in pleasure, without the least subtlety, was blowing my nose in a corner of her apron. . . . I was six years old.

Monday, April 5, 1915

My Jean is dead! He was killed March 16 in Champagne, during the attack on hill 196, near the town of Mesnil-Les-Heulus.

Sunday, April 11, 1915

Grandfather died on April 6 at 10 in the morning. So within the space of a few days, the strongest attachments of my life have received cruel blows. Grandfather was my strict, loving childhood teacher, and Jean was my childhood friend. I mourn them both at the same time, which makes the pain last that much longer.

Monday, May 23, 1915

In the evening, Valensi, Maroux, and I went walking aimlessly along the Somme. And suddenly, with no reason other than the fresh air and hunger, we were sitting at Café Ech Couco, like those sales clerks who go to small bistros in Nogent on summer evenings.

Wednesday, June 11, 1915

I've been appointed auxiliary physician and have to join the reserve health personnel at Creil to get a posting. At 3:37 A.M., I left Amiens and the field hospital with regret. Living together for ten months, developing ties that feel like habits and then the feeling of having to break them makes you understand just how much they're worth.

Sunday, June 20, 1915

My birthday. I'm 24 today. By God! The dream's over. I've been assigned to the 294th Infantry Regiment, in the 6th Battalion, not active at the moment. It's on the Haye farm in the countryside between Fouquevillers and Hébuterne. The assistant master warrant officer and I share a very comfortable, well-protected underground room. Above my head are three layers of logs, four meters of earth, and some buckled sheet metal.

I'm getting hold of Gaston Couté's patois poetry and the illustrated book, *The Temptation of Saint Anthony,* by Odilon Redon.

Monday, June 21, 1915

Tonight my mind is troubled by confused desires, vague aspirations. Is it because I've taken a break and come out of my hole, under a mist-covered moon? Funny, aren't they, the nostalgic and lyrical musings of an assistant physician from the trenches on a moonlit evening?

Wednesday, June 23, 1915

This morning I thought it was all over. I was in a back alley. I paused for a second, long enough to shake the hand of somebody passing by. A German shell exploded right above me against the edge of a parapet, about three feet away. I had just enough time to duck. I was covered with dirt and slightly wounded by the explosion. It came from a 105! Nothing more! I found the copper detonator. Some clever soldier can make me an inkwell out of it. One day I'll dip my pen in it and honestly and modestly recount to my descendants the story of my pathetic existence as a French doughboy from the Lorraine.

Louise Hunebelle

THERE FERNAND'S DIARY ENDED: with a broken promise to write his memoirs someday. I have wondered about that abrupt stop on Wednesday, June 23, 1915. He remained in service until the summer of 1917. Did an accident prevent him from writing, or did he start writing in another notebook that was lost on the battlefield? I have no answer to these questions. Nor will I ever know the identity of "little Gour all icy" who came to brighten the sad existence of a doughboy one snowy night.

It could be that he merely got tired of recording memories about the exhausting marches and encampments, day after gloomy day. I imagine that summer day in 1917, as he thumbed through some books, sunning himself in some trench, when a shell suddenly ripped through his left thigh, ending his service as an auxiliary physician. He was immediately sent back to Paris, to the Lycée Buffon, a school where a temporary hospital had been set up. There he fell into the arms of his nurse, Louise Hunebelle, a meeting that soon enough signaled the end of his youth.

I often think of my grandmother. When I was a child and feeling bored, I went to visit her. Confined to her bed, she had set to work reading the *Famous Five* series by Enid Blyton, with help from a thick magnifying glass, simply so she could give me the pleasure of commenting on the adventures of my heroes. She could relate to almost anything and was deeply curious, discussing theology as enthusiastically with her Communist friend P. J. as she did romantic problems with her night nurses. "Finish your studies and earn your living. It's the key to happiness," she kept telling the young American girls recruited from the nearby cultural center to stay in the room next to hers in case she fell at night.

Such beliefs in freedom and independence for women were puzzling from someone who had devoted her life to her husband. I wondered whether, if she'd had money and a job, her life would have been any different. To listen to her, life with Fernand had been perfect. A host of evidence indicates the contrary.

I often wondered what went through the mind of that young girl from a good family with every expectation of a peaceful and happy marriage, yet impulsively deciding to marry a penniless unknown with a somewhat thin curriculum vitae. Were his gentle eyes and passionate curiosity enough to convince her?

They married on July 3, 1919. During the ceremony, an elegant-looking man with a chest full of medals wept like a fountain watching Louise embrace Fernand. This man was worth a chateau in Burgandy, several hundreds of acres of vineyards, and a few million gold francs. My grandmother, however, had no regrets. Only one person was worthy of her—the one she had freely chosen. Moreover, at thirty-three, she had always done what she wanted. As meticulous as she was headstrong, she was adroit as a sparring partner, which certainly didn't displease Fernand. Fierce about the causes in which she believed, articulate about her literary tastes, spiritual whims, and religious resentments, she led a whirlwind of a life.

Such incorrigible rebelliousness had been a trait since childhood, when she had once announced to her dumbfounded parents that she would never marry and wanted instead to become an actress, musician, or priest (well, a nun, although that was too minor a role for her tastes). She studied at the Chevalier School (an exclusive school at the time) and early on showed a gift for music. She trained in Gregorian chant at the Schola Cantorum, where she met Vincent d'Indy, Henri Sauguet, and Erik Satie. Audacious, acerbic, and irresistibly good-hearted, the only thing she shared with her twin sister, Jeanne, was a tendency to catch the same disease at the same time (right up into advanced age). The more practical-minded Jeanne married a brilliant cartographer, Pierre Caron, and had two children by the time she was thirty-three; Louise continued to lead her nonconformist existence. She was fond of dressing up like a man. It would have been hard for anyone to have predicted what this free-spirited woman's future would bring.

Her mother, Gabrielle, was indifferent to Louise's eccentricities; she had too many other things to worry about. Since the death of her husband, Victor Hunebelle, the quality of the family life had been steadily deteriorating. With a younger brother who was as amiable as he was lazy, a daughter married to a penniless historian, and a second daughter trying to become a singer, Gabrielle struggled to make ends meet. The family was far from that golden age when the three Hunebelle brothers—Alfred, Louis, and Edouard—had built the sewers of Paris as well as a large part of the French railway system, filling the family coffers with gold. Forced to leave their home on the posh rue Pierre-Nicole, Gabrielle moved with her twin daughters and son-in-law into a rented ground-floor apartment on rue du Dragon.

Living in a room above her children, the old lady pined away, bitterly contemplating the vestiges of her past: a few period pieces that had survived the move, some dusty seashells from Mauritius, where she had spent her first sixteen years, and a photo of her taken by

Nadar when she arrived in Paris. She remembered that happy time when, bedazzled, she first set eyes on the city. She had come with the infants Louise and Jeanne in two braided baskets and accompanied by some Indian attendants. That magic time hadn't lasted long. By fifty she had become old and sour, condemned to remember a time when the sun always shone on her golden tresses.

Unlike her mother, Louise refused to live with her head in the sand or allow herself to be eaten away by bitterness and regret. She dreamed of broader horizons, a heady future. Every evening she shut herself up in her room with *World Geography* by Elisée Reclus. She felt a need to align herself with a great cause, to lead a wonderfully dangerous life aflame with international intrigue. But what could a young girl from a good family, brought up to expect a happy marriage, really hope to do?

What she could do was sing at the top of her lungs, and with extraordinary power. Her Gregorian chant teachers would have shaken their heads in amazement had they known about the reservoir of passion seething inside Louise. She had kept it well hidden. Rather than pretty, she looked fresh-faced and simple—with frank, pale blue, lashless eyes. You would not have suspected that violent emotions were stewing within.

When World War I began, Louise felt she had been offered a divine mission. The wounded needed her, and she would heed their call. She put on a nurse's uniform with the same earnestness with which she would have taken vows, and prepared to dedicate her life to healing war victims. She let Gabrielle and Jeanne leave for Normandy—in 1914, a German occupation of Paris seemed imminent—and remained behind on rue du Dragon with her brother-in-law. They were prepared for a lengthy siege. The experience of war proved far more grueling than Louise had ever expected—whatever her dreams and boasts, the truth was that her delicate hands were uncalloused. Even those hardened by life were shaken by the sight of the men dying of gangrene and tetanus as they howled with pain.

At first the chief medical officer of the hospital set up in the Lycée Buffon mistook Louise for one of those Red Cross socialites who fainted at the sight of pus and whose ministrations were limited to herb teas, ointments, and sweet sentiments. My grandmother quickly proved she was made of sterner stuff. The smell of death didn't faze her. Because she never balked at any task and was always cheerful, she rapidly became one of the star nurses. After several months she was given the responsibility of caring for soldiers with psychological problems. Far more than washing or bandaging mutilated bodies, this involved tending to ravaged psyches. Her kindness and her simple, direct manner performed miracles. And this was how she met her husband.

Fernand arrived at the hospital at Buffon on June 10, 1917, and stayed in the intensive care ward for three months while the gaping shrapnel wound in his thigh slowly healed. Though his leg was mending, he was sunk in a deep depression. His bearded face grew progressively thinner, and he lay on his back in a deep, ominous silence. Louise was immediately attracted to him. Without even realizing it, she began spending more and more time at his bedside, using a change of bandages or the need to take his temperature as a pretext to speak to him and hold his hand. She felt an emotion she had never experienced before, delighting her but also frightening her, as if she were giving in to happiness that in some irrevocable way would also bring hardship.

Separated by social class, education, and moral code, they made an unlikely couple, yet nothing could keep them apart. Fernand immediately sensed that there was something commanding about Louise; she had a life force he couldn't resist. After he left the hospital, Fernand moved into Louise's apartment. A few months before they were married, he was awarded the Croix de Guerre, and Louise given a gold medal for her devotion to the wounded. They spent their honeymoon touring around Alsace (lately returned to French hands) on borrowed bicycles because neither had a penny. Louise delightedly devoured the tartes and other local specialties, and every evening—to keep her hair healthy, she said—she poured a glass of plum brandy mixed with egg over her head. Cycling from little town to little town, they felt as if the world was theirs and began to dream about the future.

The Age of Reason

THE DELIVERY BEGAN BADLY. Her head buried under the covers, her hair plastered to her forehead, Louise let out little shrieks; her face was disfigured with pain. As soon as labor had started, Fernand sensed that things were not going well. Unable to sit still, he paced back and forth in the living room with knitted brows while the midwives bustled in and out of his wife's room, carrying basins, bowls, boiled water, ethyl alcohol, and other pharmaceuticals.

"In sorrow thou shalt bring forth children." If God existed, wondered Fernand, how could He have been capable of such a condemnation? He could hear deep, plaintive moans coming from behind the door. Louise was calling him. Feeling woozy, he sat at the edge of her bed and palpated her enormous belly. She clung to him, gripped by increasingly violent waves of pain that seemed to crush her from within. He sat there, helpless, watching her agony.

"Get the chloroform ready," barked the attending physician, Louis Dubrisay. "Hurry! We're going to have to set up a version."

Setting up a version meant turning the fetus so that it was positioned correctly for birth. That meant it was in the wrong position. Fernand watched Dubrisay proceed with calm determination. He knew that

Louise was, literally, in the best hands possible. Dubrisay had studied with Stéphane Tarnier and Jean-Paul Bar and done his internship at the Hôtel-Dieu Hospital, where he worked under Adrien Proust, coauthor of one of the most famous textbooks on obstetrics. Dubrisay had hands of gold, capable of the most daring obstetrical feats. Fernand mopped his brow. There was really nothing to fear, yet he also knew that version always poses dangers to the mother, particularly that of rupturing the uterus. An icy shiver ran down his spine. Dubrisay was surely aware of the risk.

Unable to remain in this torture chamber any longer, Fernand stood up, went into the living room, and sank onto the little plum-colored sofa that Louise liked so much. The atmosphere in the room was nearly as stifling as in Louise's room. He could almost feel the disapproving gaze of his mother-in-law from behind the door—the silent accusation that it was because of him that her daughter was suffering. It was too much. He needed some air. Forgetting his hat, he went out.

When he reached the street he began to run, running until he was out of breath. People turned and stared, taking him for another mental cripple from the war. When he got to Saint-Germain-des-Prés, he stopped to catch his breath, then simply began walking wherever his feet led him. Bloody images of the childbirth struggle churned in his mind. What would he do if Louise died? His mother, Berthe, had died a year before, followed a few months later by Madeleine Gutmann. Louise was his last support, yet all he could do to prove his love was to run from her agony. He was sickened by his own cowardice. If he'd had a bottle of wine he would have sat on the street and drunk it with the other lowlifes. He didn't deserve Louise's purity—he deserved the Pigalle whores.

It was almost two in the morning. A respectable-looking couple coming up the boulevard Saint-Marcel crossed the street to avoid him. When he got to Saint-Anne Church he stopped, staring at the entrance to the Ship of Fools Café across the street. Instinctively he headed for the café.

The Ship of Fools was a hangout for medical students. As soon as he entered, Lamaze spied Joseph Lévy-Valensi, whom he had known during the war. As usual, Lévy-Valensi was surrounded by an entourage of admirers. The topic of discussion was the gruesome crimes committed by a notorious killer named Marcel Redureau.

"Do you really think Redureau felt any remorse whatever when he lopped off his boss's head with a billhook? Do you think his conscience was at all bothered when he ripped open the belly of that pregnant woman, or when he smashed the skulls, splintered the spines, or slashed the faces of his family? Was all this premeditated or an act of insanity? That's the big question—deciding what the defendant's mental state was at the moment of the crime. Anger, jealousy, hate. Crime is man's dark way of expressing passionate emotion."

"Shut up, Joseph. You're getting boring," said the café owner. He had apparently been listening to Lévi-Valensi outline his theories about criminal behavior for longer than he could stomach.

Glasses clinked; it was like a party. Then suddenly everyone fell silent when they saw the pale face of the man standing near the entrance.

"Fernand! What are you doing here?" Lévy-Valensi asked his friend in a concerned voice. "Any decent man wouldn't go out on the night his wife's in labor. Hey, I'm just teasing. Come over. Have a drink with us."

Fernand sat down without saying a word. He felt miles away from his raucous friends with their rude jokes and one-upmanship banter. Lévy-Valensi was the most brilliant of them, as Fernand had learned during the war. Out of the forty-two men at the field hospital where he and Lévy-Valensi had worked, they were the only republicans.

The rest were royalists. Aside from their shared political convictions, Fernand and Joseph had other things in common, including a passion for history and literature. They had become fast friends. Fernand admired Joseph, who was twelve years older than he was, not so much because of his medical career—which had not really gotten on track yet—but because of his sticking stubbornly to the difficult path he had chosen, neurology. Joseph had an inquisitive, polyglot mind, which seemed open to every kind of thought. After his studies in Marseille, Joseph had had to overcome one obstacle after another; he was determined to succeed in medicine's most difficult field. Although his sharp tongue had kept him from obtaining an internship, he never gave up, not because he was ambitious but because he felt it was in the order of things for him to succeed.

In 1919 Lévy-Valensi had been assigned to the Hôtel-Dieu Hospital, where he had begun working with tuberculosis patients while continuing to study nervous trauma—shell shock—caused by the war. As if that wasn't enough, he spent his evenings working on future fields of study: spiritism and its relationship to madness; the historical (probably hereditary) psychopathological defects of the Bourbons; and his masterpiece, an exhaustive catalog of crimes of passion.

Attracted to his new friend's energy, Fernand went everywhere under Joseph's protective wing, accompanying him on his hospital visits and reading rough drafts of his papers. They had gotten to know each other so well that one would have thought they were brothers. Joseph had inspired Fernand to invent his own vocation: a doctor of souls.

In 1922 Fernand had dedicated his thesis on neurology, "A Contribution to the Study of Autonomic Reflexes of the Medulla in Friedreich's Disease," to his friend. Based on clinical observation performed under the tutelage of Gustave Roussy, the thesis reexamined the works of Nikolaus Friedreich and Jean-Martin Charcot to show how motor coordination problems developed, usually during puberty, from a hereditary predisposition, and could strike several members of the same family.

But at that moment, sitting in the Ship of Fools, Fernand was feeling very sorry for himself. He felt he didn't deserve to be linked with such medical luminaries. He had already finished off two bottles of red wine by himself. How wonderful everything had seemed when Lévy-Valensi first introduced him to Roussy, under whose sway Fernand had immediately fallen. Roussy was already world-famous for his brilliant work on the hypothalamus and its disorders, and had struggled mightily with the government to found a hospital for cancer at Villejuif. Roussy had encouraged Fernand to go into neurology and permitted him to work under him for a few months. This in turn had given Fernand the opportunity to meet the legendary Augusta Klumke Déjérine, an American woman who in 1886 had overcome the prejudices of the entire French medical community, and the disapproval of hospital's director, and become the first female intern.

Gradually but inexorably, Fernand had felt more and more distanced from the inner circle of neurology. Beset by domestic and financial worries, he had come to realize that he would have to abandon the field and seek new and more immediate sources of income. His choices were limited.

Feeling thoroughly depressed, he rose to his feet and teetered toward the café door, leaving Lévy-Valensi and his crowd behind. He knew more clearly than ever that they would take different paths in medicine.

He somehow managed to make it home. Looking defeated and bedraggled, he arrived at daybreak in the courtyard of number 21, just as the concierge was taking out the trash. Fernand avoided her critical gaze and climbed the stairs to his apartment. Gabrielle was waiting for him when he opened the door. Rather than scolding him, she hugged him tenderly. By her expression he could see she was glad to see he was alive.

"She's waiting for you."

He entered Louise's room. The curtains were closed, and it took a moment for his eyes to adjust to the dim light. As he approached the bed, he could see his wife sleeping peacefully. On her stomach was a little ball of moving flesh. He came nearer and touched the child's head, as if to convince himself of its existence. Soundlessly, it opened its mouth wide and began crawling toward its mother's breast. All Fernand could feel was deeply tired. Suddenly a hand was on his shoulder. Dubrisay was standing behind him.

"Come into the living room where we can talk."

Fernand followed him, his head bowed, as if he were about to hear his death sentence.

Ignoring his foul breath and the state of his clothing, Dubrisay summed up the delivery.

"The child's doing well. A beautiful six-and-a-half-pound girl. And not at all deformed, which is a miracle. But her mother's been badly hurt. She needs to rest. Fernand, pull yourself together. This is no time to go on a bender. Now show me the bathroom, will you?"

Lamaze lead Dubrisay to the bathroom. While he washed his hands, the doctor continued giving Fernand details about the delivery and explained what should now happen. Dubrisay was a slender, serious man who at first appeared off-putting but who underneath was generous and kind. He had one of the best clienteles in Paris and was well known for his skill and his humanity. But the war had taken its toll on him, as it had on so many others, and he was preparing himself for retirement.

Dubrisay dried his hands and began putting his instruments into a large black case. Then, with Lamaze trailing behind him, he began pacing around the living room, silently examining objects and touching the fabric on the furniture. The couches were worn, the chairs were chipped, and the paint on the walls was beginning to flake. The apartment was furnished in good taste, yet everything indicated financial straits. When he had finished his methodical inspection, Dubrisay turned to face Fernand.

"Well, young man, now is the time for you to start thinking seriously about your future. Like you, it took me a long time to choose a field. My father was a member of the Council of Health and Hospitals, ready to help me in any way he could. He urged me to go into surgery. Obstetrics never even crossed my mind. It was looked upon as a backwater profession. Women's labor was considered purely a physiological function and without any fundamental connection to science. I took people's word for this, until one day I attended a frail, exhausted-looking woman who was going into labor. The midwife was late, and the woman was at the end of her rope. I had to perform the delivery alone. I had no experience. Medical school had only offered us theory. But I threw myself into what was one of the most meaningful experiences of my life. Believe me, romantic intimacy pales in comparison to the bond an obstetrician feels with a woman in labor. You become a creator. You are given the chance to give life, to bring a human being out of the depths and into the light.

"Now I will stop lecturing you and move on to serious things. Show me your hands."

Dubrisay seized Fernand by the forearms and carefully examined his hands. He scrutinized every inch of skin, studied the veins, tested the flexibility of the wrists and the dexterity of each finger.

"Your hands give you away. There's no escaping them. Come see me tomorrow at my office."

Such went the conversation that would forever change my grandfather's life.

PART THREE

STORIES WITHIN STORIES

He let himself become convinced that human be-ings aren't just born once, when their mother gives them life; but that life makes them give birth to themselves, quite often, again and again.

—GABRIEL GARCÍA MÁRQUEZ
Love in the Time of Cholera

The Gift of Life

FERNAND'S COMMITMENT TO his new career grew quietly but steadily. Having agonized about what field of medicine to choose, suddenly the choice had been made for him, and he gave himself to it. Louis Dubrisay had been right: obstetrics was a perfect fit. Fernand moved easily and naturally into his new role and saw the act of childbirth through from beginning to end. He stayed by the bedside of the woman giving birth, guiding her through that mysterious metamorphosis of her body, breathing with her, putting himself as close as he could to her suffering until the crowning moment was achieved.

Fernand the nonbeliever had been touched by grace—redeemed by the gift of life—and he gloried in it. Within ten years he had earned a reputation for being the best obstetrician in Paris; requests for consultations came in from across France and across Europe. Despite his radical politics, he became the doctor of choice for denizens of the poshest neighborhoods. Some began to wonder how a doctor with left-wing leanings, a doctor who did all his own work rather than delegate it to underlings, could become the darling of high society. Malicious tongues wagged. Fernand soon became aware that success bred enemies. And what they couldn't forgive was his love for his work and his apparent lack of interest in profit or glory. In these ten years of practice, he had never raised his fees, and his skillfulness meant he did far fewer costly episiotomies (surgical enlargement of the vulva during labor) and cesarians: "Perform cesarians for free, and you will soon see that there will be fewer of them done" was one of his favorite phrases. Another was "Place your faith in the perineum, and it will live up to it."

One spring morning, on his way to see a patient, he sat down for a few moments on a bench in Furstenberg Square. He loved this particular bench, and when he was in the neighborhood he always found time to sit on it. On this day Fernand was in a serious, reflective mood, but enjoying the feeling of the morning sun on his face. Mme Vaisse's delivery had gone well despite the position of the fetus. The delivery had taken all night; at dawn, he had placed a sturdy 8-pound-4-ounce boy on her belly. This was Mme Vaisse's fourth boy, and she was already thirty-nine years old. The next time, he knew, he would have to convince her to give birth at the hospital. As she got older the risks multiplied. People's habits, however, were hard to change.

He took a tube of glycerine out of his bag and rubbed some on his hands, studying them carefully. The years had not altered them much. They were still as tapered and sensitive and smooth as they had always been. He fluttered his fingers in the air, like a pianist practicing on an imaginary piano, while a homeless man watched him with amusement; he already knew about the doctor's eccentricities. Suddenly checking his watch, Fernand realized he had less than half an hour to get across the city, and got up to find a taxi.

He had never learned to drive a car, an inability of which he was enormously proud and satisfied, for he was convinced that steering wheels were the obstetrician's worst enemies. Among other evils, they created calluses and permanently stiff wrists. He would have chosen to ride to the poorhouse in a taxi rather than risk damaging his hands.

Thinking about the first years of his career brought a smile to his face. He and Louise had no money, and he had had to set up his office in their already cramped apartment. It was impossible to move around the apartment without passing through the waiting room or stumbling into a patient. Despite all this, they had stayed put.

Because they lacked the means to hire assistants, Louise rolled up her sleeves and learned to do everything: she worked as the receptionist, made the appointments, paid the bills, and did the cooking—the Lamaze table was always open to guests, and some would arrive without a moment's notice. Whenever he saw her bending over the books and struggling to make ends meet, Fernand felt stabs of guilt. The life he had chosen had turned the romantic young girl he married into an overworked secretary. He knew he was responsible, but also found a way to blame her. It should have been obvious to her that he didn't deserve her love.

He bought a newspaper on boulevard Saint-Germain and got into a gray Mercedes. He told the driver to take him to Vincennes Hospital. The ride lulled him. Closing his eyes, he thought again about how fate had forced him to abandon neurology and turn to obstetrics. As far as the medical community was concerned, obstetricians were mere technicians; all they did was help a simple physiological function to occur. At medical school, the course in obstetrics met once a week, and at the end of the year the students stood behind barriers in the hospital's main lecture hall to witness an actual delivery.

Fernand had therefore had no real experience when he began accompanying Louis Dubrisay to all his appointments. He had acted as Dubrisay's assistant, and from the beginning the idea was that the professor would hand over his practice to Fernand when he retired.

All Fernand could remember of those first experiences was the nauseating odor of placenta and the terrifying rictus of women in labor.

One evening in the winter of 1924, Fernand received an emergency summons to the home of one of Dubrisay's patients, whose contractions had begun a month before the baby was due. She lived on the ground floor of an apartment building with a poorly lit courtyard. The midwife was already there and had unpacked the instruments, prepared the bowls, and boiled the water. Apparently no one else was at home—no husband, siblings, mother, mother-in-law. Fernand approached the woman and began to palpate her belly. The woman grimaced in pain; sweat had glued her hair to her temples. She yanked the covers to her chin and made little shrieks of pain while the midwife began mixing a solution over some burning alcohol.

Sitting on the edge of the bed, Fernand cautiously began his examination. The woman opened her eyes and began to shriek even louder, clutching the sheets with even greater force. Labor had already begun. "A breech," the midwife whispered in his ear, as if he had not already surmised that the fetus was in the wrong position.

Trying hard not to panic, Fernand focused his thoughts on what Dubrisay would do in this situation. Why was he late? Matters couldn't wait. The only recourse was to use what was called the Mauriceau maneuver, as refined by Louis Faraboeuf and Henri Varnier. You located the fetus's mouth while pushing your forearm against its body—it was as if the fetus were on horseback. The fingers of your other hand braced its neck. Doing this within the woman's narrow pelvis was extraordinarily difficult—and meant risking accidentally rupturing the uterus. The pain, in any case, would be excruciating.

Perspiration flowed down Fernand's back. His hands were clammy. The midwife watched him anxiously as she prepared the chloroform. He knew there was no choice, and knowing this immediately calmed him. Dubrisay was always careful, but once he decided on a course of action he worked quickly and confidently. Fernand placed the chloroform mask on the woman's face and watched the liquid drip onto it. He remembered what Dubrisay had told him: "When using chloroform as sedation, have the woman breathe several drops at the start of each contraction, then stop as soon as the contraction is over." The chloroform seemed to be working; the woman's features relaxed slightly. Fernand silently offered praise to Queen Victoria, who at the time of her last labor in 1853 had asked her doctors for the analgesic. But suddenly the woman began to shriek so loudly that her voice sounded inhuman. It was as if all the suffering in the world were swooping down and would overwhelm them both. Suddenly he could feel, to the tips of his fingers, what the woman was feeling. Waves of pain and anger rolled through his body.

The struggle lasted the entire night. When dawn came, he began applying small lateral movements to the child's head, and at long last it emerged. Fernand knew he had changed during the course of that night; he was no longer the same man. In his journal, he noted tersely: "February 3, 1924, 7 AM. Have finally lost my virginity."

From that day forward, childbirth became more than his profession; it became his obsession. He dedicated his days, nights, and waking thoughts to it. He even dreamed about it. In one recurring dream he would arrive at the hospital feeling as if his feet were dragging but his body was light as air. The nurses and doctors greeted him, but rather than leading him to his office they took him to the waiting room and sat him down among the pregnant women. The door was closed; no one spoke. They all shared the same secret. Encapsulated in their bodies, which were like perfect spheres, they were listening to something within them, absorbed by the life forming inside them, the growing power that would transform them into the creators of the world.

Fernand often wondered why men had been denied the gift of

life. It seemed to him an unacceptable inequality. And it was because of that sense of exclusion that he was driven to understand the process, to participate in it as fully as he could, to get as close as possible to the mystery of it all. He engaged all his empathic powers to catch every echo.

Few of Fernand's colleagues could understand the passion with which he threw himself into his work. They, too, were obstetricians—but could as easily have been engineers or bankers. They believed they were in a game in which all the cards had already been dealt. Why make labor painless when God Himself had deemed otherwise? "In sorrow thou shalt bring forth children" suited their indifference perfectly. They built their power base on a temple of obstetrics that was blind and deaf to women's suffering.

Only a revolution would change the medical status quo and establish the basis for a new way of looking at obstretics. Fortunately for Fernand, a small group of doctors were thinking in those terms, and during his internship he had been lucky enough to meet one among them. Louis Funck-Brentano, the son of a well-known economist, was director of obstetrics at Salpêtrière Hospital. An avid student of art and opera, he was a sensitive soul deeply concerned about women's health, and had decided that diminishing a pregnant woman's anxiety and suffering during labor could help increase the birth rate. Though his colleagues opposed it, he employed whenever possible the anesthetics and analgesics that were then available in France. Funck-Brentano and Lamaze frequently bemoaned the poverty of means at their disposal. Injecting cocaine into the spinal column was dangerous; shots of morphine-scopolamine worked but often intoxicated the mother, had serious side effects, and, worst of all, diminished contractions. All that was left was chloroform, which was both relatively ineffective and could prove harmful; because it passed from the mother to her fetus—you could detect the odor of ether in the newborn—it could lead to hemorrhaging and death. Well into the twentieth century, though medicine was progressing by leaps and bounds, obstetrics seemed mired in the Middle Ages.

The taxi passed by Hôtel-Dieu Hospital. Fernand's heart sank at the sight of this grim institution, a fortress filled with disadvantaged women, consumptives, outcasts, teenage mothers, those who had had abortions. Puerperal fever, went the rumor, was rampant here, ravaging mothers and their babies. As if that weren't demoralizing enough, there was another rumor that each woman was forced to wear a gown with a number stamped on the front and give birth in a common room that resounded with screams.

As in all rumors there was a grain of truth to all this. The atmosphere at Hôtel-Dieu did seem unwholesome. But Fernand also knew from experience that its maternity ward was extremely well run, employing the latest hygienic techniques, and that it had an excellent track record in the use of analgesics. He and others believed the rumors had been started by midwives, who saw the modernization of childbirth as threatening to their livelihoods and fought it by spreading false information. Good Catholics, they believed the only place for a woman to have a baby was in the sanctity of the home. A motherless home is one bound for temptation and sin. Fernand found it difficult to fight such ignorance and still maintain his focus. The hostility and vituperation tended to undo him. He didn't know how to react to it, how to keep it from overwhelming his life.

The taxi came to a stop in front of Vincennes Hospital. Fernand glanced at his schedule. This appointment would last until 5 P.M.; he had to be at Belvédère Hospital at 6; at 8 P.M. he was to visit Madame Henri, who was suffering from a fever; at 10, written in pencil in tiny letters, as if from some deep shyness, was the name Rose. He would have to lie to Louise again.

Louise's Diary

Friday, August 19, 1938

I gave myself permission to take up my pen today. I don't intend to make this diary a trash heap for all my resentments. I just want it to contain some of the things that are too heavy for me to bear alone.

It's six in the morning. I'm in the garden at Grosrouvre. I love that place more than anywhere else. We bought this old farm barely two years ago. According to the village legend, it once belonged to Diane de Poitiers. But was I here in a former life? I get the feeling of always having lived here. Every corner of it, decorated by the previous owner, is just what I would have liked: enormous libraries where Fernand has finally been able to find room for his treasures; big rooms with bay windows that have a view of the garden, a ground-floor kitchen, its door always open for friends who stop by to chat when I'm trying out a new recipe; and way up on top, on the roof, the "blue room," which has the power to give your dreams a very special depth, and from where the out-of-tune organ can be heard throughout the entire house.

We've just celebrated Anne-Marie's fifteenth birthday. For her, and in tribute to her beauty, I filled all the vases with flowers cut from the garden—peonies, lupine, and roses. Fernand's thirty guests couldn't believe their eyes when she appeared dressed up like a sultan. She looked so pretty, with her face framed by a turban—more like a Madonna than Scheherazade. For once her father didn't hide his feelings and, filled with emotion, took her in his arms. By midnight the party was going strong. The art of cuisine really brings people together. I think my lobsters with paprika, my *truffles à la serviette,* my Scottish hazel grouses, and my vanilla soufflé with an exceptional Sauterne made life seem not that bad at all.

After the pear brandy, Fernand lit his pipe and recited three hundred verses of the *Légende des siècles* [*The Legend of the Centuries*] by heart. He was exultant. Jeanne LeBey Taillis, Emile, Jean and Alice Gutmann, Pierre Brisson, Françoise Rouchaud, France de Ganey, Bernard Vaudoyer with his inevitable Evelyne, Pierre Rouquès and the leading lights of the medical world were all with us, their eyes shining with admiration.

Who would have dreamed of such a rapid, smashing success? In about ten years, Fernand has become the best-known obstetrician in Paris. And I, the little nurse who married the good doctor, dare to complain! What a shaky couple we are. I can hear evil tongues hiss as I go by. After the party, my good mood vanished, and I stood in front of the empty plates and withered flowers with a tight throat, my eyes full of tears, feeling as if I wanted to evaporate like the morning dew.

"Our hearts are like the trees of Arabia, the more you crush them, the more incense pours from them." How completely Bossuet understood the human soul, because a heart purged by pain knows a whole other kind of passion. Despite what he's put me through, I love Fernand more than ever.

Sunday, August 21, 1938

Back in Paris. It's raining, the sky uniformly gray and low. Everything is sad and cold and empty and futile. To have faith and then just wait, bearing it all. Today's gray, heavy, indefinably gloomy sky makes me better understand what sacrifice is.

Tuesday, August 23, 1938

The world is being ravaged. The pigs are making treaties with each other. General Vuillemin has left for Berlin for endless discussions with Chancellor Hitler and to admire the buffaloes being raised by General Goering in his private park. It's like a dream! And I'm silly enough to moan about my little problems. I reread the first lines of this diary and they sound like some religious nut weepingly contemplating her navel as she patiently waits for absolution.

Wednesday, August 24, 1938

Finally, some good news. The British cyclist Lilian Dredge has done 1,000 miles in 4 days and 18 hours. Now the stronger sex isn't the only one breaking long-standing records. Fernand burst out laughing when I showed him that male hegemony was in its last hours. During these affectionate little quarrels we go back to our former closeness. But such moments are getting rarer and rarer.

I remember that night at the Pleyel Auditorium on May 9, 1921. I was singing Handel's "The Nightingale" and Fernand had come to applaud. I didn't know it would be my last concert, but I did better than I'd ever done, just to please the man I loved. The audience clapped wildly. I realized what an amazing impact the human voice can have. It's a magical organ that can defy earthly forces, turning your body into a taut, vibrating bow. I soared over the world, full of love as if it were some divine mission. Maybe our marriage was a kind of aberration, but it was one hundred percent a matter of the heart. I have no fortune and I'm not descended from anyone in the world of medicine. Whereas others married their supervisor's daughter, Fernand decided to marry a penniless singer, who, besides having a rotten character, has a mouth candid enough to make him fall out with the whole world.

Thursday, August 25, 1938

Fernand was and is my only love. At the beginning of our marriage, I spent my days thinking about him, looking for any pretext whatsoever to get close to him, smell him, inhale the pages of books he'd paged through a few moments before, lovingly empty the ashes from his pipe. All of it must have seemed laughable, and sometimes I couldn't keep from shaking when I thought that I'd end up like those old fools who worshipfully knot the scarf of their indifferent husband as he nods off—their excessive devotion having put out what's left of the flame.

That was how I lived: awash in bliss, immune to any care that might darken my marriage. However, there was one detail that preoccupied me and that was the lack of passion Fernand showed in bed. He finished quickly, using my body as if it were only a receptacle for his own desire. Since I had little experience in the business of sex I figured that such cursory groping must be the rule and that the heavy passion and arousal I'd been dreaming about was just a figment of my imagination. Still, a slight bitterness about it only got worse over the years.

Anne-Marie's birth ravaged my body like an earthquake. I was permanently damaged by it, but I was so fulfilled by what nature had given me that those two nights of suffering are still the most beautiful moments of my life.

A few months after my daughter was born, I lost my singing voice. Its range was different, and its strength was destroyed. That beautiful organ was dead. Now I had only one goal: to help Fernand find fulfillment and become a great doctor. Now that he's at his peak, am I still useful to him?

Sunday, August 28, 1938

Mme Thibault's baby was stillborn. Fernand wouldn't touch his dinner and has shut himself up in his room to sob. When I see him in that state, my heart melts; I'd do anything to console him. That must be one of the reasons why we've lasted so long together. I'm the only one who knows about his fits of weakness, which he hides carefully under a gruff exterior. I'm the only one who really understands him. Lots of times I've wanted to walk out, but just seeing him at night hiding his grief, overwhelmed by the suffering he's been so close to all day, and my resentment disappears; I stay at his side.

Friday, September 2, 1938

Today, delivered Mme Docet's baby at Belvédère, 3 P.M. Then at 8 P.M., Dr. Noir's daughter, at Vincennes. Tomorrow, Countess de Saporta at Mme de la Panouse's. Then, at 4 P.M., Mme de Saint-André, the sister-in-law of Mme Hémond, at Geoffroy-Saint-Hilaire Hospital.

After I did the accounts, I went bargain hunting with my friend Marguerite Cancalon. We've known each other since school days. We have so little in common but we adore each other. She's about as worldly and affected as I am natural and disinterested in my appearance. But what I love about her is her hunger for freedom, her total absence of conformity. On our way to rue Drouot, where the paper had announced a sale of Chinese porcelain from the Ming to the Daoguang periods, she told me the latest news about the Celveland murderer. They think he's already responsible for eleven crimes and is probably familiar with surgery, a doctor, in other words, who uses his knowledge to perpetrate the worst horrors. Maybe he's a good, attentive, considerate husband who suddenly reveals himself without any warning. You think you know a man, and then all of a sudden you discover you have been living with a monster.

A crowd of well-to-dos was pushing to get into this temple of knickknacks. We ran into Mme Champetier de Ribes wearing a daring cocked hat with peacock feathers. That cinched it for Marguerite; she rushed up to the second floor. With a hint of irony, I left her to her "Chinese shadow play," hoping she wouldn't lose too much money, and went down to the ground floor. Here an auctioneer was trying to push some moth-eaten stuff. There was something sad about the place, like an unused theater full of mismatched furnishings. Only faded lace, torn lingerie, and yellowed silk fans remained as vestiges of a life in the dust.

Despite the morbid atmosphere, I've always loved rummaging in thrift shops and second-hand stores. I feel like a hunting dog, sniffing under the rags and rot for hidden treasures. Quite often I've paid a few hundred sous for something worth more than a thousand, some collector's piece lost among the chipped saucers and paste jewelry.

This time at Drouot the hunt was less fruitful. My haul included an espresso spoon, a bust of Napoleon, a kerosene lamp, a swath of corduroy, and a clock that doesn't work but has a fascinating mechanism. Emile Gutmann will love it.

Marguerite was bursting with pride when we left, until I told her that the Ming porcelain she'd bought at the price of gold came straight from the workshop of an excellent forger. I thought that our friendship was going to end right then and there, but a glass of warm wine at the café on the corner reconciled us. If only love could be as simple as friendship. . . .

Saturday, September 3
Spent the afternoon on the Champs-Elysées looking for a winter coat. At Toutmain's there was a fantastic one in the window, completely lined, with a black astrakhan collar, reduced from three hundred fifty to two hundred francs. That evening, when Fernand saw

me all got up at Lipp, pouring with sweat under my new purchase, he burst out laughing. It's obvious that elegance isn't my forte!

We got home at midnight with full bellies, as we do every Saturday, happy to have eaten our usual *saveloy* with mustard sauce and that delicious *mille-feuilles* pastry at Marcelin Cazes'. Sometimes I tell myself that eating well is the last thing that keeps Fernand with me. Meals are the only times when we're together as we used to be.

I still remember our first meal. It was at a rundown café in Les Halles run by a couple of former students who knew Fernand when he was in school. At 3 in the morning, he challenged me to eat a big plate of noodles with lard, a triple consommé with quenelles, and, to top it off, potatoes *à la barigoule,* which he loves. When I ordered dessert, I knew I'd won his heart. The next morning he asked me to marry him.

Sunday, September 4, 1938

Dinner at rue du Dragon. Of course, Emile Gutmann was there; Ortiz, who was just named head of the Foreign Legion; old Freyer; André Weill, who boasts about being an anarchist; and the Jahouanns, our fishmonger friends from Les Halles. They all got on famously. At 8 P.M., Fernand put on his big soldier's overcoat and went down to the cellar to get his best bottles. It's a ceremony that he especially likes to perform. He puts a quasi-religious ardor into it, getting ready as if he's going to mass. Birthdays, family or patriotic occasions, my heathen of a husband punctuates his life with rituals! Really something to think about. . . .

Monday, September 5, 1938

M. Seyer is suspiciously eager to accompany his wife to all her doctor's appointments. He's the husband most involved in consultations at rue du Dragon. The game he's playing is so obvious that you'd have to be blind like Fernand not to notice. While his wife is being examined, he leaves the waiting room and knocks timidly on my door. The poor man always shows up when I'm plugging away at the accounts! His eyes looking like a beaten dog's, he sits next to me and gets down to the business of courting me. His favorite adjective is "disarming." He keeps stuttering it: My innocence and candor are disarming. In other words, I'm a naive little thing! Next, after these psychological insights, he moves on to describe my anatomy: my velvety skin, rosy coloring, the delicacy of my ankles and wrists, my wasp waist, even my feet deserve praise! I have a hard time not bursting out laughing. If I were a little bit mean, I'd use him to get my husband jealous. But I hate cuddling females and emotional blackmail. Love isn't negotiable.

Tuesday, September 6, 1938

We were invited to dinner at the Funck-Brentano's where we met the head of Baudelocque Hospital, Alexandre Couvelaire. What an odious man! When I think that he's the son-in-law of the great Adolphe Pinard—and also his successor! During the meal he declared in his falsetto that suffering valorized women. He thinks a woman giving birth has a "moral beauty," and he went on at length about the stoic will of those mothers who "procreate in tears and blood for the country." How can such idiocies come out of someone's mouth! He's also one of those hypocrites who, in the name of God, systematically sacrifices mothers by doing cesarians in extremis, to save the little soul from the womb. "Life comes first," they have the nerve to say, using God as an alibi for their own cruelty!

I've often discussed the problem of pain with Fernand. If it's inevitable, then it has to be accepted completely. But saving yourself and others from suffering is always a way of offering glory to God, since according to creation's design, the greatness of man comes from his mastery over nature. Man should do everything in his power to fight suffering. Every moment of Fernand's life is directed toward this fight.

Unfortunately, he's not getting much support from his colleagues. Some reply that the curse God put on Eve, "In sorrow thou shalt bring forth children," can't be violated. Others react sarcastically, and accuse him of misplaced concern: "It's an easy form of suffering; as soon as it's over, you laugh about it." "Millions of people throughout the world are in agony; you would do better, dear Lamaze, to concern yourself with raising the birth rate and thinking about the sufferings of our poor country, which was bled dry by the war." As if one kind of suffering rules out the other!

If we could destroy prejudices about childbirth and prove that pain isn't inevitable, that would already be one victory for humanity; but these narrow minds can't break the yoke of convention.

Saturday, October 1, 1938

I haven't written in my diary for nearly a month. Because of laziness? Definitely. But also because I'm ambivalent and weak-willed and because I dread looking truth in the face. What happened during this time? Not much that merits mentioning here, a host of little tasks that break up and parcel out my days, making them end late in the evening, in the nothingness of a refreshing, imbecilic sleep. Around us the world's in a dither. At Nuremberg, Hitler's spreading hate with his "brownshirts," 140,000 arrogant, brutal men hammering the ground in cadence, ready to crush anything in their way. In the face of what's happening over there, our worries seem truly insignificant. At the end of the day, Blanche Selva and Marguerite Cancalon came by for tea, and each tried to boost my morale with totally opposite arguments: praying, according to Blanche, or getting a lover, according to Marguerite, will cure all my ills.

My two friends are so different yet so close to me that I often begin to imagine that they're the double incarnation of my soul. Blanche Selva, Anne-Marie's godmother, is obese and mystical and transcends her ugliness by playing piano with a nearly divine gracefulness. Marguerite Cancalon is thin and atheistic and backs up her principles by boasting about her affair with Georges Robert, the director of the Société des Gens de Lettres. I've often heard about the legend of the Double. If you ever meet your spitting image, you must face death. When my two halves meet, will I finally have earned the right to rest?

Sunday, October 2, 1938

Dinner at the Gutmann's. I'd worn what I had lying around and had had to endure Gabrielle's usual rude remarks: "A man is something that has to be earned; you won't keep your husband by decking yourself out like that." What a pest! Fernand loves me the way I am, and Emile has thanked me a thousand times for that writing desk I unearthed for him at the flea market.

Wednesday, October 5, 1938

Recently one of our friends, a doctor in Lorraine, went to Hawaii. He told us that over there women go through labor naturally, with a smile on their face. They're stunned when they hear the colonial women screaming. If that's true, then pain isn't a constitutional necessity. The story had a deep effect on Fernand. From it he came to the conclusion that pain could be a cultural phenomenon and that the more refined a country becomes, the more difficult childbirth is. But what can be done about it? Sometimes Fernand reminds me of

Sisyphus tirelessly climbing back up the slope, crushed by his rock. What if he were to finally let himself slide to the bottom and be happy with obscurity and retirement?

Monday, October 24, 1938

Last night was the unveiling of the Monument to Mothers on Boulevard Kellermann. All the self-righteous of France gathered around the sculpture by Bouchard and Décatoire, a gigantic, hideous fresco to the glory of the progenitor. The battle for the birth rate has taken a grotesque turn. It started with special bonuses for deserving mothers. Then came prizes for them (Cognacq-Jay promised to give 25,000 francs to 100 families with 9 children); and now they've created medals: bronze for 5 children, silver for 8, vermeil for 10. Where will it end? Soon women will be branded as they leave the maternity ward! Such stupidity leads me to agree with the positions taken by Jeanne and Eugène Humbert. Although I'm not a Malthusian as they are, I do believe that procreation has to be a conscious, well-considered act, so that each child will play his deserved role within the family circle.

The unspeakable Mme Couvreur represented Catholic midwives and presided over the unveiling. I'll only cite a few sentences of her speech: "Nowadays women don't want to suffer and make more children. But having children is a blood tax, the price you must pay to honor your country. We must ignite and maintain in young women the flame that only religious sentiment creates by teaching them to find their suffering sacred."

I had a hard time keeping Fernand from expressing his rage; the two of us left, like two thieves, in the middle of her speech, mingling with the parade of old soldiers and schoolchildren.

Wednesday, October 26, 1938

Dinner at the Vaudoyer's, rue du Dragon. Evelyne Galleron stared at me during the entire meal. I felt absurd in my little hat with a veil and my mauve-colored tunic dress, which I'd been so proud of until this evening. But I'd lost the battle in advance. Compared to Evelyne, every woman looks like a peasant. She cultivates a casual look, at the same time choosing the cleverest cuts of fashion. Most important, she knows how to keep up a reserved, modest exterior, all the while exciting men with every batting of an eyelash or movement of her hands.

Luckily, Jeanne Le Bey Taillis was there, supporting me just by her presence. It would take an entire novel to tell the story of the life of that courageous woman who, after a disastrous marriage, slowly made a comeback using her talent for the game of chess. More than anything, I like that parable about wasted talents, and I think there's no greater sin than letting what God gave you at birth lie fallow. But Jeanne has not only exploited her genius for chess moves, she's also made it profitable. She's now the head of the Caïssa Chess Circle which she just founded, and she does battle with the Tartakovers and other chess geniuses at Café de la Régence. Chess, that misogynist stronghold, won't ever recover from it!

After dinner, I caught a gleam of triumph in Evelyne Galleron's eyes. Fernand seemed embarrassed. I pretended I hadn't seen their little exchange. At home, I locked myself in the bathroom, looked at myself in the mirror, and cried.

I went to bed with a red nose. Fernand was already asleep. He was lying across the bed, taking up all the room. I got in as best I could. I couldn't stand the sound of his breathing, but I had no other place to go. I began thinking how I'd like to become a street acrobat, a juggler, or a fire-eater, and then leave the scene doing cartwheels.

Saturday, October 29, 1938

My sister called me. Her husband is in line to become director of the National Archives. Such a promotion would crown the brilliant career he's had so far as a cartographer. For my sister, it would also be sweet revenge, after all she suffered at the beginning of their relationship. I often think about our teenage years when we duped our admirers at the ball by switching identities. We'd switch partners and listen to the steamy intentions they had in mind for the "other." Twinhood is a strange story that comes to an end only when you die. However, today I feel we're not as close as we were and that life insidiously has warped our features, little by little, directing our actions away from that path that leads back to our communal beginnings. I'd promised Jeanne that I'd never lie to her, that I'd always be a faithful echo of her. If only she could read my mind now and see all the secrets weighing it down!

Maybe one day I'll put down here the words that I don't dare say out loud in this diary. Only Jeanne could understand them.

Thursday, November 3, 1938

Fernand has gotten wind of a decree being prepared by the government that would allow doctors to alert the police if they learned an abortion had taken place. What a horrendous method! The times are about informing and putting to death.

Yesterday we went to the Detoeuf's for dinner. Fernand didn't say a word. I learned afterward that Mme Vernand had lost her son.

Thursday, November 3, 1938

Read a strange story in *Le Figaro*. A buffalo that lived in the zoo in Vincennes for twenty years suddenly went berserk and gored its keeper. As he had every day, the keeper came to bring the animal bales of hay that were scattered on the ground. All of a sudden, the buffalo rushed toward him and killed him.

Why had he rebelled like that after so many years of submission? Isn't that the inevitable response of any prisoner toward his jailer, despite the show of trust between the two?

Sunday, November 6, 1938

We recently heard about someone named Read who practices "childbirth without fear" in England. According to him, the climate in which a woman gives birth can play a noxious role and increase the pains of labor. His method must be causing quite an outcry over there and earning him the wrath of the Anglican Church. In France, it's more a question of complete indifference.

Tuesday, November 8, 1938

Fernand is away more and more. He dines alone at the Detoeuf's with Pierre Brisson and his sister, Françoise Rouchaud. I met her husband, André Rouchaud, at a concert where I was singing a Schubert lieder. He'd come up to say hello and heaped compliments upon me. Now that my voice is ruined, my presence is less sought at society dinners.

I'm having trouble understanding what Fernand is looking for among these people so socially and politically distant from us. His uncouth, peasant side must get a smile out of all those grand bourgeois.

We argued this evening and he left without even kissing me. I dared to make a remark about our money disappearing as if we had holes in our pockets, and to say that buying the house in Grosrouvre had put quite a strain on our budget. But he didn't want to hear anything about it.

Friday, November 11, 1938

The troops have marched by. Drums and trumpets before a crowd of happy, uncaring rubberneckers. Meanwhile, Jews are being hunted in Germany, synagogues are being burned down. Is man the only creature that lets himself be blinded so easily?

I abandoned Fernand to the fanfare and stayed home, still reeling from yesterday evening. Thursday had been busy. Fernand was tense, ready to explode. He finally took it out on poor Anne-Marie. Her crime was daring to cross the waiting room to get to the bathroom. What else was she supposed to do in this quirky apartment! Stay closeted in our rooms all day?

The evening ended in shouts and tears because Fernand thought it was a good idea while he was at it to give his daughter a definitive no about going to the Conservatory of Music. Mme Lebout, her piano professor, and Mme Hinstin, Emile Gutmann's cousin, however, came over last week to beg him to give in to his daughter. The little girl is gifted, but that doesn't mean much to him; he sticks to his position. Anne-Marie will finish school and won't become an "entertainer" like her mother. Why is he so rigid? It's hard for me to admit it, but the person whom all Paris praises as a humanist devoted to the cause of women is nothing more than a domestic tyrant!

What hurts me the most about this is my mother Gabrielle's obsequious attitude: "Don't fight your husband's decision. You have to know how to give in. Getting on your high horse all the time won't help you keep Fernand. You'd do better to keep an eye on him a bit, and to finally open your eyes, rather than playing at being a virago."

After having injected her venom, my mother went up to her room without even paying attention to my tears. The evil had been done. What I'd dimly sensed without admitting suddenly took form and showed itself in the light of day. Fernand was cheating on me. He'd always been cheating on me. I'd been stupid enough to want to deny the evidence and Gabrielle, secretly jubilant, put me back on the right track and opened my eyes to my misery.

As for misery, she's wallowed in it all her life, and now it seems right to her for me to join the long line of wounded, sacrificing women. How many times has she told me the story of her placid life as a young girl on Mauritius, before someone came to steal away her sixteen years? Just as in a bad soap opera, what comes next is a series of catastrophes: an unsuccessful marriage, ruin, then illness. At forty, her husband, Victor Hunebelle, became impotent and turned into an infirm, obese hypochondriac, condemning Gabrielle to live chained to him, like the prisoner in the Minotaur's labyrinth. Victor's death wasn't even a deliverance since one ends up getting used to one's misery. It can sometimes even become the driving force of your life. And my mother, whose life is ruled by an immense loneliness, has no other option than dwelling on her sorrows and killing all hope in me.

Saturday, November 12, 1938

Is it this inability to face reality that makes [my mother] close to Fernand? Everything ought to separate them, but every day they become closer. They share the same exile and I remain alone, even more alone.

Monday, November 14, 1938

Fernand was out all night. He came back at dawn. I pretended to be asleep when he slipped into bed.

Thursday, December 1, 1938

Anne-Marie has a primary infection. It was detected during a medical visit at Maupre Hospital. There's a very good chance that it's tuberculosis. I leave with her tonight for Duretol, where she'll get care. Fernand is devastated and in shock.

We'll go at night. Before we leave, I'll make dinner for Fernand—salted pork and lentils and an apple pie, like the kind they eat in Alsace. I made a list of things he should do on his desk. His appointment book had a letter written in violet ink used as a bookmark. I didn't have the courage to read it. It's better that way.

Nostalgia and Its Risks

MY GRANDMOTHER'S UNFINISHED DIARY had arrived one morning at the post office on rue de l'Université. It was as if it were an echo of the one by Fernand I had found a few weeks before. In the package containing it was a prayer book and the birth certificate of the Hunebelle twins, accompanied by a short note to me from Jacques Caron, my mother's first cousin:

Dear Caroline,

I heard you were doing research on Uncle Fernand. These documents I found after Jeanne died might give you some clues for a better understanding of him. But don't forget: if your grandmother's life was governed by a will to clarity, Fernand's was made up of shadows and mysteries. Sometimes it's better to let darkness do its work than to illuminate the past with lights that are bound to be misleading. But I'm sure you have your own ideas about this issue.

Fondly,

Jacques

I wondered what he meant by this. I also wondered how Jacques had found out that I was interested in the life of my grandfather. And why this obviously private diary found its way into his mother's apartment. Perhaps Louise had given it to her sister because she was afraid her husband would see it.

Whatever path these pages had followed, reading them I was overwhelmed with emotions. The suffering they expressed seemed so out of character with the gracious, angelic old lady who had enchanted me as a child. I never detected a particle of grief in her smooth face, perpetually lit up by a smile that had the power of making life seem carefree and fun.

After I read them, I was placed in a different world. The day dragged by. I paced in circles, incapable of doing anything—not even opening the door and taking the dog out for a walk.

How is youth measured? I have a fleeting memory of waking up one morning in Grosrouvre, the house of my childhood. I rushed to open the big window through which sunlight streamed, sure that the day would bring wonderful things.

The moment doubts and second thoughts creep in and breathing grows heavy, the game is over. That is when nostalgia seems like the only way to survive. I have often given in to it like a vice, and after my initial anger at what I found in Louise's diary, I began to find things in it that fed that vice. Buried memories crept to the surface; names I thought I'd forgotten became familiar again, slowly reconstituting a landscape with contours so precise that the real world seemed to lose its shape.

Fragments cohered. The chess champion, Jeanne Le Bey Taillis— was she not the same old lady my mother used to visit in the hospital? Blanche Selva, kneeling before a cross; Marguerite Cancalon, holding a white poodle; Mme Rouchaud, swimming in a pond in Holland. Whether I had seen these things or only heard of them didn't matter.

I took refuge in the past, which became a protective bubble; names I had heard growing up assumed a kind of incantatory virtue. There were moments of ominous silence—the "blanks" in my grandmother's diary, her secrets. Who was this arrogant Evelyne? I thought she was probably my grandfather's mistress. Was she the author of the letter in violet ink that served as a bookmark for his appointment book, or had another of his admirers sent it to him? Where, I wondered, did this "great humanist" find his female quarry? Among his patients, perhaps. The physical intimacy between obstetrician and patient seems destined to lead to a different kind of relationship.

I struggled with a series of unanswerable questions and indulged in wild hypotheses, as if I personally had been a victim of my grandfather's sins. Late that evening, when I suddenly realized I was hungry and discovered that the refrigerator was empty, then noticed that my poor neglected dog had deposited two conscientiously arranged turds on the Persian rug in the living room, the silliness of my reflections became apparent. Furious with myself, I went out to buy some food along boulevard Saint-Germain-des Prés, which has been destroyed by clothing stores. Nothing was open. The only thing left to do was go to bed.

Sleeping did me no good, proving the stupidity of the adage that says it heals all, and I woke up feeling even more anxious than I had felt the night before. It was all so absurd. I was torn up by jealousy over a man I had never even known. What right did I have to stick my nose into the affairs of dead relatives, when my own life was so far from admirable?

I knew someone who might help answer some of my questions—Jacques, my Grandmother Louise's nephew. I resolved to call him, and yet for some reason kept delaying actually dialing his number. He was a pediatrician, and from childhood I had been intimidated by him. I was told that when I was a baby I used to howl whenever we went to his apartment on rue Jacob. I remember that as a teenager I used to feel nervous when I climbed the 120 steps (I had counted them) to his office. The front doorbell was rung by a long green cord covered with yellow spots shaped like the eyes of peacock feathers. It looked like a snake. Sitting in the waiting room the minutes seemed like hours, until finally a handsome, strapping man with a mischievous look on his face emerged from behind the red velvet curtain that hid the door to his office. I would start to feel faint. His teasing didn't help. I dreaded him far more than his shots. At the end of the appointment he offered me the box of candy reserved for younger children. Despite my "advanced" age, I always guiltily gave in to my weakness for candy, though I knew my cousin was gently mocking me, and noting which piece I had chosen—as if its size and shape were clues to my inner thoughts.

At home my parents often spoke of Jacques's brilliance. He had been tremendously lazy and apparently uninspired by school, but my grandfather nonetheless pushed him into medicine. Perhaps it was Fernand's contrariness that allowed him to be so taken by Jacques. The young man had everything that Lamaze lacked—charm, an ease about himself, the ability to make anyone smile. He got an internship with ease, and proved loyal to his supervisor. Unlike most doctors, Jacques was a deeply cultured man with a solid grounding in literature and history, but his greatest genius was his ability to tell jokes— an art he felt was undervalued in the world of medicine. He practiced it with high seriousness, and embraced all of its forms. His range of puns went from the backroom variety to the most refined spoonerism. He used time off to create elaborate practical jokes and was as pleased with making his victim the butt of a vulgar prank as with a sophisticated scenario. He had wasted no time turning humor into a philosophy, and saw himself as a healthily subversive force, a destroyer of sacred cows, ready to lead the charge with his wit. With age his sense of humor had softened somewhat, and I had not heard much about either Jacques or his jokes for quite a while. I picked up the phone and tried reaching him at his home, his weekend home, his favorite retreats—all without luck. I began to wonder if Louise's diary wasn't yet another of Jacques's tricks, and he was somewhere out there laughing at my gullibility.

Rather than going to work the next day, I took the day off. I felt a desperate need to get away from it all. From some sense of loyalty, I had held onto the old Renault my father had driven toward the end of his life. He had died years before, but the car was still sitting in a garage for which I paid the monthly bill; I even kept the registration and insurance up to date. Normally I hate driving and would much rather let someone else do it, but for some reason this time I wasn't at all worried. I went to the garage. The old car came back to life with a single turn of the key. An hour later I was parked in front of the gate to the farm in Grosrouvre that my grandparents had bought after the war.

Nothing had really changed, but I was immediately disappointed; it was as if the light had gotten harsher, shrinking the surrounding houses and making them seem shabbier than I had remembered. The effect was to make the horizon seem smaller and metallic. Two hideous prefabricated houses had been constructed on the cow fields, turning the otherwise pristine countryside into a Parisian suburb. The house itself proved another disappointment. The ivy had been removed and it stood naked, open to the elements and every eye.

I parked the car next to the ruins of an arch, called the Arch of Diane de Poitiers. The cornfield in which I had played with the Colet kids rustled from a light breeze. It was a mild day. The plateau was deserted. Across the street, where the Poussignots' family farm still stood, everything seemed more or less the same, and for an instant I felt as if I was ten years old again.

The new owner of the house was named Madame Hervé. She had blocked up the old kitchen door, which had opened right onto the road, probably out of fear of burglars. So I entered by the main gate. The garden was well maintained but there were no more flowers. A doll was lying on the lawn. A little girl probably lived here. I wondered whether she climbed "my" tree and enjoyed the delights of the pond and the weeping willow. A gray-haired women in a tweed suit met me at the front door. She seemed unfazed by my surprise visit and warmly invited me to take a tour of the place.

I knew that coming out here had been a mistake. One cannot reappropriate a place that has stopped being yours. My house had become unrecognizable. Antlers decorated the burlap-covered walls; the wooden ceiling beams were gone; the bay windows had been turned into security doors; a faux baroque stove stood in the center of the big room, which was no longer lined with books. I wanted to laugh and cry at the same time, but my hostess was so kind that I complimented her on how tastefully the house had been decorated. We talked a bit more. She told me that she had had the trees in the garden cut down because they were too much work. The weeping willow was gone. The Lebon boy had married a Porcher. My playmate Florence had married a schoolteacher. She had nearly died in Saint-Louis Hospital, from some kind of blood disorder. I also had been treated for the same problem in Saint-Louis two years before. Wasn't that a strange coincidence, I thought. Mme Hervé said that I was remembered for that in these parts. My parents must have been so worried. But how well I seemed to be doing now, she said, and why didn't I stay for dinner? It was getting late. I could tell that she was enjoying my company. It couldn't have been easy living alone in a big house. Her granddaughter came for a visit every couple of weeks, but nothing would replace the husband whom you had loved for twenty-five years.

Her affability began to feel stifling, so under the pretext that I had important obligations back in Paris I took my leave. Evening was falling, but I had one last visit to make before driving home.

The Shortcut

I HAD TAKEN THIS PATH hundreds of times. I loved its twists and turns, its hidden nooks, and especially those place where sunlight would suddenly blaze through the branches. I knew the path so well that I could have walked it blindfolded and in a hurry. It led up a hill to the little cemetery of Chêne Rogneux. There, above the fields and meadows, a sea of poppies at my feet, I knew I no longer had anything to fear. I could make my childhood start over again; all I had to do was rush down the slope.

I walked past the gravestones with a happy smile on my face, glancing at the half-worn inscriptions, finding names I recognized: there was the Russians' family vault, to the left of the church; the Grenaudiers' tomb was under the oak; and finally M. Rochaud's tombstone, two steps away from Fernand's. I closed my eyes, enjoying the feel of the sun's last rays. I had buried my grandmother and my father here, but the memory of both ceremonies had faded; all that remained was the music of our laughter and that light feeling of dizziness children get on a headlong run.

On the way back down the path, I met an old gentleman holding a bouquet of tulips. He said hello and presented them to me. I remembered he had been the village carpenter as well as its mayor for twelve years. He told me he had seen me at my grandmother's funeral. "A great woman, like Dr. Lamaze, who was a hell of a gentleman. The kind you don't forget." He kept repeating this.

Driving home, I thought about what the old man had said to me, probably to please me. Without really understanding why, I felt suddenly very happy, almost ready to burst out laughing. I was convinced that my search for my grandfather's story wasn't a complete waste of time after all.

When I got home, I tried to reach Jacques Caron again, but there was still no answer. I decided to continue my research. The Academy of Medicine had been closed for a week, preventing me from looking up a memoir written by one of Lamaze's contemporaries, which I was positive would shed some light on the period. Such setbacks were frustrating, though I wouldn't admit to the possibility that I was using them as excuses not to face more painful issues about Lamaze's past.

At noon on one Wednesday, I made my usual visit to Montsouris Hospital to see my mother. A rumor was circulating that she was about to be released. I felt lighthearted as I climbed the stairs, nodding to and chatting with the nurses and doctors, and greeting the patients whose faces were now familiar to me. I even thought I would miss seeing them, like someone leaving a resort at the end of the summer. As I turned a corner, I thought I recognized who else but Jacques Caron, leaving my mother's room, number 14. Was this possible? I ran toward the man but he disappeared into an elevator before I reached him.

I learned later that it had been Jacques. Besieged by curiosity, I began to bombard him with telegrams and phone calls, unsuccessfully.

I might have suspected that my cousin wasn't the sort to employ such vulgar modes of communication to impart family secrets. As the son of an archivist and historian, raised surrounded by books, he felt the spoken word was deceptive and not to be trusted. The written word alone had the power to penetrate the past and impart truth.

Truth in Lying

My dear Goddaughter,

It's taken me quite a while to pick up a pen. There were so many things I wanted to tell you, but I put off this moment as much out of laziness as out of decency.

I'm sure you've read that lovely story by [Louis] Aragon, "Le Mentir vrai" ["The True Lie"], in which the poet believes art uses lies to make truth stand out all that much more vividly. I strongly endorse this theory. Life is but one vast construction: recollections are inventions, memory but fragments of photographs badly glued together. We can only read life in dreams, which propel us toward an elsewhere that we alone control.

I've had to learn the art of lying as a matter of survival—one's own and others'. What is the point of passing hasty judgment when the truth lies hidden in a gallery of mirrors and escapes all classification and logic? One has to find a shortcut that leads one straight across the field, to use backtracks and detours, and to approach and contemplate the truth by placing it in a larger and fairer perspective.

I have done this throughout my own career. Do you think a patient truly capable of hearing the worst? Spoken at the wrong moment, the word kills.

You need to adjust the truth, almost to hedge it. Deep down a sick person is no fool, but a zone of uncertainty permits him to cling to hope. Besides, no doctor is a god. No one's prognosis is 100 percent reliable.

I sent you Louise's diary with this in mind. To put you on the right path. When I learned that you were looking into the question of Uncle Fernand, I didn't want to allow myself to be limited to the role of nice Cousin Jacques, adding one more brick to the edifice known as the great Dr. Lamaze. Family legends are the most difficult of all to prevent, for they are self-sustaining and sui generis.

Fernand would have hated seeing himself turned into a statue. This diary gives him back his life. I didn't change a single comma of it, but I chose not to send you the next part, for there was one, which I destroyed. The last pages were too dark and too hard. Your grandmother wrote them in complete despair. In their bleakness they went beyond her, and she certainly wouldn't have wanted them to dominate a portrait of her husband.

When Lamaze died, she only wanted to retain the best part of him, forcing herself to expunge the past of all its ugliness. After that, forgetting did its work, rounding out the painful angles, reestablishing the true proportions. She died with the image of a man who, despite his weaknesses, had loved only her.

Now that we've clarified this, permit me to continue Louise's story in my way.

We left off in December 1938, on that fateful day when Louise's suspicions about Fernand's infidelity were confirmed and when your mother's primary infection was diagnosed by Dr. Lévêque. As was always the case, crisis strengthened Louise, whereas it caused Fernand to collapse. A year later, he went to war in a camp near Paris, consumed by anguish and fear. Louise meanwhile sent the rest of the family to Auray, in the unoccupied Free Zone, and then returned to be with her daughter at the Duretol Sanatorium near Clermont-Ferrand. Two years passed, punctuated by brief visits from Fernand, who was busy with a growing clientele and a fairly important role in the Resistance. In

1940, when the Germans arrived, Emile Gutmann took his own life in his garden. Your father left for America with his three children and his first wife, Alice.

In 1942, Louise returned to Paris with Anne-Marie. After months of being an invalid because of a rupture of her adhesions and three attacks of pneumonia, the little girl's health seemed to be improving, and Louise came back to the fold flush with newfound hope. She now believed that the clouds over her love life would pass, and that life on rue du Dragon would return to what it had been in better days.

A terrible shock awaited her. Boasting that he had been celibate for two long years, Fernand actually believed it best to have his new mistress move into the room next to that of his mother-in-law, Gabrielle. This seemed to him the most honest and practical solution: there would be no more time lost by telling lies, no more exhausting comings and goings. He also felt that an obstetrician needed to be available to his patients; if they looked for him now, they would know where to find him.

I am convinced that if your grandmother had had a little money of her own, she would have moved out then and there. But she didn't, and so decided to stay with her incorrigible husband with whom, moreover, she was still in love. She put on a good show and, following Fernand's orders, invited to her table every other day that person known as "Mme François."

Fernand's passion for this unrefined, unattractive woman remains something of a mystery. She must have had hidden talents, it was whispered. I myself believe that she was simply a part of Fernand's barracks-room fantasies; by allowing himself to be infatuated with a slut, he would remain, in his way, faithful to Louise.

Fernand's insistence on doing things properly had made him want Mme François to be "integrated" into the family. This excessive concern for convention, an outbreak of "bourgeois-itis," disconcerted all of us. Among the paterfamilias's whims was making Anne-Marie accompany the lady to the Théâtre-

Français every Friday, and on holidays, making her sing a medley of her greatest hits after dinner.

Another of his paradoxes: Fernand forbade his daughter from attending the Conservatory because he thought it "disreputable," yet he pushed her to do shows in front of floozies.

In 1947 Mme François threw herself into the Seine after having begged Fernand in vain to get a divorce. Your grandfather was only slightly upset about it, then took two mistresses, who this time remained in their own living quarters. The first, Irène, had just gotten out of prison and worked as his chauffeur. The second, Laure Duval, was a debt-ridden hysteric whose only function was to ruin Fernand financially. He bought her an apartment in Paris and a house in Vendée.

Your grandfather had finally realized his fantasies. The little peasant from the Lorraine was at the height of his glory, feted by all of Paris, indulging in the high life like some true nineteenth-century bourgeois. Yet despite appearances, he loved only one woman—his wife. When he took Louise to Russia in 1955 for a triumphal trip consecrating the work of the Lamaze Method, I think that she finally understood that.

A flood of other memories come to mind as I write. I have so much to tell you. There was that time when Louise went to Balzar wearing one of her extravagant little hats. Fernand, flanked by one of his "ladies," had invited me to dinner to celebrate my internship. Louise stood directly in front of us, lifted her veil, and drank her rival's entire glass while staring her straight in the eye. Then she smilingly turned on her heels and left while we stared transfixed. Fernand was gloating. He loved your grandmother's sense of humor. On the other hand, the "lady" didn't look quite so happy. She also didn't last very long.

Fernand and Louise were an astonishing couple, and when all was said and done they were deeply united. I remember them sitting at Lipp in front of delicious food, talking with Léon-Paul Fargue who, as usual, was hailing a taxi to go back to his place on rue Jacob, though it was only a few blocks away. Louise sat behind her enormous glass of beer, captivated by her husband's tales *of his imaginary walks in countries he'd never visited but knew better than anyone because of books.*

He was unrepentant, as in love with books as with women, going to extremes to find every possible outlet for his idea of freedom. One evening my father decided to take the bull by the horns and visit his brother-in-law. Once they were alone together, he timidly dared to express a few reservations about Lamaze's uneven morals. He got quite a reaction. Lamaze accused him of being a hypocritical philistine, preferring the petty pleasures of being a bourgeois adulterer to frank, honest situations. Pierre Caron came home steaming, vowing never again to get involved in his in-laws' business.

From that day on, nobody in our house was allowed to criticize Uncle Fernand's behavior. My father had understood once and for all how futile it was to oppose him.

Anyway, few risked doing so. Lamaze exuded such strength that even his worst enemies were intimidated. Talk to the men and women who met him: they all speak of his "magnetism," his gentle, casual way of winning people over to his point of view. He could hold a listener spellbound without ever using his authority and while remaining a good listener, never seeming too prejudiced or too sure of himself.

Freedom was the cause that dominated your grandfather's entire existence. He applied it to both his personal life and his professional practice. But you can't be too dismissive of conventions; little minds made sure that he paid dearly for his boldness.

When he passed sixty, your grandfather could have rested on his laurels. He had the best clientele in Paris and divided his time among the wealthy patients of Belvédère Hospital, Cours de Vincennes, Sainte-Félicité, and the hospital at Bluets founded by his friend Pierre Rouquès. Nonetheless fate was to step in: Fernand had chosen to become the bearer of a new philosophy.

I won't tell you the story of the Lamaze Method of painless childbirth in great detail. So many of the passions and symptoms of a period of history are involved that an entire book couldn't do it justice. To tell it, you would need to track down exact dates, seek out missing witnesses, plunge into minds and archives. It's a tough job; Lamaze's "psychoprophylactic method" is not only often maligned today but ignored. Nevertheless this method was profoundly innovative, a harbinger of all the struggles that were to come, all those freedoms promised and dreamed about.

It all began in 1951, in September, to be exact. Near the end of a trip to the Soviet Union, Lamaze was invited to visit the obstetric practice of a Professor Nicolaïev, in Leningrad, and witnessed the six-hour delivery of a thirty-five-year-old woman having her first child. She showed no signs of pain and remained calm and relaxed. From that day on your grandfather's life was changed profoundly. Despite hostility from the entire medical community, he became the tireless apostle of the psychoprophylactic method, which would be named for him several years later.

With the cooperation of the hospital at Bluets and financial support from the Fraternal Union of Metal Workers of the Seine, Lamaze began his mission. Drawing on theories about conditioned responses by Pavlov and Velvoski, he articulated his own methods. He based his technique on the idea that fear of pain during childbirth, inculcated for generations, creates a painful uterine contraction that can be countered by instruction in the physiology of labor and by classes in muscular relaxation. The physical and mental preparation of the pregnant woman thus consists of rational, physiological training, an appropriate respiratory response, and assuming positions that facilitate the desired muscular slackening. "There are no miracles," he wrote, "unless you are referring to magic tricks or subterfuge. The woman learns to give birth as she would learn how to swim, as she has learned to read and write, and she gives birth without pain."

This may seem naive in the era of the epidural. All current "preparation" for childbirth is, however, still based on Lamaze's precepts. And you also should bear in mind that in the fifties, most women didn't know their bodies very well and had accepted the notion that suffering was divinely sanctioned.

Even women with more sophisticated views saw pain as nature's warning of some danger hidden deep inside them. Ridding them of pain by making them actively involved in childbirth and removing a millennium of passivity required a veritable psychological revolution.

The Lamaze Method was immensely successful—very quickly and despite attacks from colleagues. The Blue Bell Girls, Madame Prévert, the American actress Deanna Durbin—women from all around the world wanted to have their child delivered by Lamaze. In January 1956, the pope recognized the method. [The actor Jean] Gabin came to consult with your grandfather before the filming of "The Case of Dr. Laurent." Doctors and midwives from the world over went to Bluets Hospital to do internships. Lamaze's story is the story of an extraordinary clinical adventure, and to tell it you would have to describe how Bluets went from being a hospital for workers to becoming an international center. You would have to bring back to life the atmosphere of those years. But who today could do that?

Lamaze is a great figure in French medicine. He must not be allowed to sink into oblivion. He belongs in the line of Pierre Budin, Stéphane Tarnier, Baudelocque, Pinard, to all of whom we're indebted for the medicalization of childbirth. He deserves to be rediscovered and revived; there are shadowy areas that need to be illuminated. The mystery of his death should be examined, since I, as well as my friend Henri-François Rey, believe that he was done in by enemies from within. Someone needs to talk with the last surviving witnesses, sift through the evidence, turn the memories inside out the way you would a pocket, find the solution to the puzzle.

If you think I'm the man to do it, you're mistaken. I'm not good for much of anything anymore; my memory is failing. No matter how much time I spend each day lying on my back with my feet propped up against the wall above my head, in an attempt to get the blood to irrigate my brain, the memories return only to go rolling into the pit of oblivion.

Moreover, actors shouldn't recount their own story. I knew Lamaze well and liked him too much to be impartial or to be able to untangle all the threads. But you're both close to him and distant at the same time, far enough away to see the meaning of his life. Don't waste time.

Affectionately,
Jacques Caron

Prosper Lamaze: A man of order and habit, who taught his son to take the high road of national service and avoid the side streets.

Gabrielle Hunebelle: The old lady pined away, bitterly contemplating the vestiges of her past: some dusty sea shells from Mauritius and a photo of her taken by Nadar when she arrived in Paris.

Young Fernand Lamaze with his family: You can read the toil and sweat in this family of peasants from the Lorraine, who are proud of having hoisted themselves by their own bootstraps to the rank of teachers.

Louise in her nurse's outfit: As meticulous as she was headstrong, there was also a little bit of the sparring partner in her that certainly didn't displease Fernand.

Emile Gutmann: Their friendship lasted nearly thirty years, ending a month before the Germans arrived in Paris, on May 19, 1940, which was Emile's birthday and also the day he chose to kill himself.

Lamaze during World War I: Lamaze the field medic is cultivating a new image: doomed angel.

Anne-Marie Lamaze (*left*): Who is that young, provocative woman bending toward the camera lens, bursting into laughter?

Jean Gutmann (*right*): Everything about him spoke of the charmer: his innocent, devastating blue eyes; a distinguished, devil-may-care side to him, set off by little details.

A young Jacques Caron with his "master," Fernand Lamaze, in the garden at rue du Dragon. Gabrielle (*center*) keeps an eye on things.

Lamaze in his office: Crammed with books, this room looked more like a researcher's study than a doctor's office.

Lamaze during his trip to the Soviet Union, in a children's garden with Professor Weill-Hallé.

Lamaze explaining the birth process to mothers-to-be.

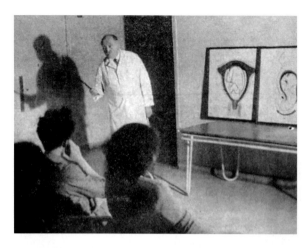

LA REVUE
des travailleuses

C.G.T. REVUE MENSUELLE — N° 12 — JUIN-JUILLET 1953 F.S.M.

Oui !...
J'ai accouché sans douleur

Thanks to Francis Crémieux's recording, women can practice the Lamaze method at home.

During the last trimester of pregnancy, the husband should monitor the exercises.

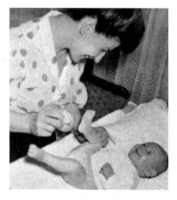

Three seconds after her birth, she's already doing a recording with PATHÉ-MARCONI.

Lamaze dedicating his book to the town of Saint-Denis. Behind him, the mayor, August Gillot.

Dr FERNAND LAMAZE

Qu'est-ce que
L'ACCOUCHEMENT
SANS DOULEUR ?

AITRE • SAVOIR ET CONNAITRE • SA

Fernand Lamaze's book: Published in 1956, this manual would become the bible for generations of women.

The Pierre-Rouquès Metal-Workers Hospital in the 1950s.

Lamaze holding actress Deanna Durbin's daughter. The Lamaze method was immensely successful...women from all around the world wanted to have their child delivered by Lamaze.

Pour le docteur Lamaze un des deux pères de ma fille.

En Amitié Heureuse

Jacques Prevert

After Jacques Prévert's daughter was born, he did this dedication for Lamaze: For Doctor Lamaze, one of the two fathers of my daughter. With warm regards, Jacques Prevert.

Bringing a Ghost to Life

SPRAWLED OUT ON THE COUCH in my apartment, I leafed through Izis Bidermanas's photography book on Paris. The poet Jacques Prévert had written the text for the book, which he had inscribed to my grandfather—"To Dr. Lamaze, one of my daughter's two fathers." Sitting on the coffee table in front of me was a copy of Prévert's *Paroles,* a beautiful edition bound in black velvet done especially for my grandfather. The book had always fascinated me. When I was young I often took it to school for show-and-tell, mostly out of sheer family pride—but also to earn the admiration of my teachers and maybe improve my grades.

Photographs filed past my eyes as I flipped through Izis's book: horse-drawn carriages covered in snow; flower girls standing in the vast emptiness of the Gare de l'Est train station; shadows from gas lamps reflecting on walls covered with peeling posters; faces of children peering from behind broken windows. On one page Prévert had done a kind of Surrealist collage for my grandfather's amusement. Across the roofs of Paris, magnificently photographed by Izis, he had drawn a figure in green ink busily scribbling a letter. Gigantic green leaves spewed out of chimneys: "To Fernand Lamaze, in happy memory of the birth of my grandchild—fragile, tiny, and perfect."

I looked out my window and saw it was nearly dark. "Don't waste time," my cousin had warned me when I told him I was writing a book on my grandfather. Yet how can anyone who is writing a biography avoid wasting time? How do you get beyond the process of gathering together the pieces of a person's life, a process that prevents any one aspect of that life from truly coming alive. My cousin's letter was a cruel reminder.

"He spent the first part of his life dreaming about what he would do with the second, and the second part regretting what he hadn't done in the first." Where had I read it before?

Jacques was right. It was time to get to work. I had wasted enough energy beating around bushes and gathering wool, seizing on whatever scattered biographical tidbits about the great Fernand Lamaze came to hand, accumulating notes from the bottomless bibliographies at the School and Academy of Medicine. It was time to end the preliminaries and get down to the real business of giving life to a ghost.

I went back to flipping through the Izis book when suddenly a particular photo caught my eye. It was of a little girl with a doll-like face and large blonde curls. She was sitting on a wooden horse. The camera had caught her slightly turned away, unaware of the camera's presence. She seemed to be lost in the intensity of the moment. She was beautiful. Her skin was radiant. So real was her pleasure that she seemed about to spring off the page.

> *A passerby stopped*
> *In front of the birth announcements*
> *And marveled*
> *A traveling salesman of images*
> *And without knowing it*
> *A traveling musician*
> *Who plays in his own way*

Especially in Winter
The Rites of Spring.

The question was, How could I too become a "traveling salesman of images" and give flesh and bone to the grandfather I never even knew? All the reading I had done to this point had given me only a partial sketch. What I needed now was to meet Fernand Lamaze—not face-to-face, of course, but indirectly, the way a pool player sometimes uses a third ball to sink his target in the pocket.

As far as talking with family members who knew my grandfather, I could run down the list of immediate survivors pretty quickly. On the Hunebelle side of the family—my maternal grandmother's side—there was of course my mother as well as my cousin Jacques and—if I could find out where she was—the daughter of Great Uncle Pierre, my grandmother's brother. I hoped she was still alive. Following the lines of my grandmother's genealogy, however, meant running the risk of getting sidetracked into writing a saga about the Hunebelles. As I've said before, they deserve a saga, one that would give a full account of how they built the French railroads and sewers and went to live on the Mauritius islands—but that would be a different book.

The other genealogical line I could follow was on the Gutmann side, my father's family. I knew that my half-brother Pierre had lots of Grandfather Emile's letters and papers; he had often spoken to me about them. But again, the danger was getting sidetracked.

The last part of my plan was to take a trip down to the Vosges region to go through the archives at Vincey and de Mirecourt. The part of Fernand Lamaze's life that seemed fuzziest to me was the period between World War I and II. Madame Detoeuf, August's daughter-in-law, could probably clarify the relationship between Lamaze and the Brisson family. The daughters of Joseph Lévy-Valensi, who died during deportation to a concentration camp, had continued to correspond with our family; it would be simple enough to look them up and interview them. There was also someone whose life I would have loved to have learned more about, someone who played a critical role in the life of the Lamaze family, and this was Jeanne Le Bey Taillis, the sister of my grandfather's best friend and the founder of the legendary Caïssa Chess Club. She died in obscurity in 1970. I wondered if her chess club was still going. For the war period itself I would need to rely on a colleague of my grandfather's named Professor Paul Milliez and whatever help he could provide to make clearer my grandfather's part in the Resistance.

If information about Lamaze's life before the war seemed scattered, what was available about his activities in the 1950s, when he was fighting the battles for his "painless childbirth movement," was infinitely more plentiful. There was an enormous pile of documents: articles from the press, books written about or by the famous Dr. Lamaze, copies of lectures he had given throughout the world. Pierre Vellay and other former colleagues at Bluets Hospital could tell me about the final chapter in my grandfather's life, his final days as leader of the movement he had founded and to which he devoted his life.

I closed my eyes, my conscience soothed by the idea that I knew now what lay ahead. My plan seemed perfect. I had "quartered" my subject, reordering the facts of my grandfather's life around comprehensive chronological axes that revealed both thematic unities and biographical interconnections.

My apartment suddenly seemed stiflingly hot. I opened a window. The last clients from the restaurant across the street were tumbling out into the street in noisy confusion. Not a breath of breeze; the moon was bright and troubling in its fullness. Tired as I was, I decided to delay going to bed, and picked up the recording that Fernand Lamaze had made in 1955, two years before his death.

On the back of the record jacket were a series of photographs that mapped the process of painless childbirth. In one you could see my grandfather, wearing his white lab coat, standing before a group of young women and using a pointer to draw their attention to a diagram on the blackboard. The diagram involved dilation. Then there was a photo of a couple walking in the predawn hours. "Two hours before checking into the clinic," read the caption. Finally, at the very bottom of the record jacket, was the key to the whole thing: a newborn pictured howling into a microphone. "Just three seconds after her birth, she is recorded for posterity."

I put the 33 LP on my mother's ancient record player. There came the sound of scratches and static, then my grandfather's voice: "Painless childbirth using the experimental psychoprophylactic method involves the physical and psychological education of the pregnant woman during the final months of her pregnancy. Its primary focus is the abolishment of the so-called 'divinely decreed' pain associated with the contractions of the uterus during labor. The painless childbirth method requires no medication, has no unwanted side effects, and involves absolutely no risk either for the mother or the child."

The record skipped and jumped, yet my grandfather's voice sounded forceful and convincing—carried along by a kind of serene steadiness. The Copernican Revolution of painless childbirth had taken dominion.

I knew then that my plan of action for writing my grandfather's biography was pathetically wrong. No one's life can be divided into tiny chronological slices. And Fernand Lamaze's entire existence had been formed at that moment when he realized there was a way of making people's entry into the world what he also wished for the lives they went on to lead: painless.

The War Years

FRENCH CHESS GRANDMISTRESS Chantal Chaudé de Silans inherited the Caïssa Chess Circle from Jeanne Le Bey Taillis. I managed to track down her whereabouts through a bookseller friend who also happened to be a good chess player. Through him, I was invited to the former French champion's home, where the club now met.

After my visit to Chaudé de Silans, my head was swimming. Although seventy-seven years old, a veteran of battles against the greatest chess geniuses of her time, she seemed as fresh and enthusiastic as a young girl. Her life would make a wonderful novel. However, this venerable lady told me nothing about Jeanne Le Bey Taillis that I didn't already know—Le Bey Taillis's chaotic love life in Nancy; the divorce that sent her to Paris looking for work; her dramatic rise from the basements of the Café des Variétés to the drawing rooms of Faubourg Saint-Honoré, when the club was at the peak of its popularity and power. I had also already known the outlines of Le Bey Taillis's rapid descent into poverty and obscurity, and how she finally ended up in the charity ward of the Hôtel-Dieu Hospital.

About Fernand and Louise, Chaudé de Silans had had only a few memories. There was one, however, that she told me she would never forget. It was of my grandmother's melodramatic arrival at Caïssa during a chess tournament. Her hat was tilted sideways and her cheeks were aflame. Alarmed by her appearance, Jeanne left the game for a few minutes, an infraction of the rules hazarded for only the most serious of reasons. Mme de Silans never learned what Jeanne and Louise talked about.

I had already met over a dozen people who had known Lamaze, either casually or closely, and each time I experienced the same disappointment. These meetings were always interesting—Lamaze's name seemed to open doors—and sometimes they were quite moving, but inevitably I left them feeling frustrated. Hardly would a memory about Lamaze surface when their minds seemed to start skidding, and with it the thread of their story. Perhaps I had expected too much. As Jacques had reminded me, truth doesn't come neatly packaged but in fragments. What I most needed was some distance from it all, so that I could arrange the broken pieces of the past. The process reminded me of my Latin homework. I remember you used to begin by doing a literal translation, figuring out all the parts of speech, and then unraveling the logic of meaning. It was so easy to make mistakes. Therefore, cautiously, I began to construct a picture of my grandfather's life between 1940 and 1950.

The year 1940 began with two funerals. As soon as the war started, Lamaze lost his two best friends. On May 19, Emile Gutmann took his own life in his garden, celebrating his birthday with this radical act of nose-thumbing at the German invaders. A few months later, his old friend Lévy-Valensi was deported to the concentration camp at Drancy. Joseph had stayed too long out in the open, believing until the end that the Vichy government would save him for the services he had rendered his country.

In both cases, Lamaze had been helpless to save his friends. His frequent urgings to Lévy-Valensi to leave France were countered by an optimism that was as unshakable as the pessimism with which Emile reacted to Lamaze's advice. Moreover, the banker had already lost his illusions about the state of the world, and French society in particular. On November 29, 1938, he had sent a very strong letter to France's chief rabbi, who had written an article in a newspaper calling for a Franco-German rapprochement in order to maintain the peace. "One cannot believe that a French rabbi would admit publicly to such cowardice. One is filled with anger. It makes one want to chase the disgraceful priest from the temple."

By December 31, 1939, Emile Gutmann was already planning his death, as we see in a letter he wrote Lamaze:

Time to sacrifice one's life? It doesn't seem so. Instead we're trying to destroy the enemy by other means—blockades, planes, propaganda, etc., all kinds of things that when it comes down to it won't have the same effect occupying land does. The Germans are wrong, but they've conquered Polish territory and by so doing proved that they are right and the Polish are wrong—about this, at least. Meanwhile, the Allies, who have it over everyone else in terms of manpower, minds, raw materials, machines, wealth, and communications, think time and patience will prove them right. Can you really vanquish the enemy without attacking him? Can you get someone to change merely by trying to frighten him with propaganda, or by isolating him, or by denying him food? The impulse to enjoy life's pleasures—and thus to save your own skin—has created complacency. It all makes me think of the decline of Rome, which little by little began to balk at waging wars, and hired legions of mercenaries to defend its immense empire. I send you these thoughts at the start of a new year, one too many years for an old man like me who will soon enough pass on.

Your faithful friend,

Emile

Emile had been a faithful friend to Lamaze but was not faithful enough to stay with him while France collapsed.

In 1940 Jean Gutmann chose to depart by different means. On November 1 he and his family went to the United States, after a terrifying period of being on the run. The Gutmanns spent long hours waiting outside the American consulate in Marseilles, located on a coastal road and near an edenic park perched above the Mediterranean. They were part of a miserable crowd of people who had trudged there hoping to obtain an exit visa. After that had followed endless negotiations with the Vichy government in an attempt to get a second French visa by way of Wiesbaden. Panic reigned in the port cities. A fleet of boats waited in vain for sailing orders that never arrived; motorboat tickets were bought with gold by wealthy foreigners—but the rides never materialized. This was the nightmare my father lived, caught in a trap that was quickly closing in upon him. The Vichy government first prevented liners from leaving French harbors, then prohibited all French citizens from leaving the country by plane. At long last, after having been ripped off by smugglers, fleeced of most of his money, and nearly murdered in a cornfield, he made his way to Portugal, where he joined the rest of the family and left for America.

With the last of the Gutmanns gone, Lamaze became an orphan of his adopted family. He came to the conclusion that there was nothing and no one left to live for and allowed himself to sink into a depression from which even the energetic Louise could not lift him. The cowardly acts perpetrated by Vichy sickened him. He felt he had been personally corrupted by his country's abdication, dirtied by the hate that seemed to have poisoned France's finest minds. The false judgments and hypocrisies undermined the one guiding principle of his life—respect for freedom and human dignity.

All the members of the Lamaze family opposed Marshall Pétain and his Vichy government. Fernand's father, Prosper, was the most vocal, though he never stopped idolizing Pétain, the great hero of World War I. Instead of causing the family to fall apart, however, the war brought the clan closer together—bonded by their disgust and rebellion. Louise seemed to have gotten twenty years younger. Every day brought a new struggle, and she was proud of all her little acts of bravery against the "filthy beast"—getting up to give her seat on the subway to a passenger wearing a yellow star, spitting when a German soldier walked past, ripping up the flowers planted by the collaborationist concierge in the courtyard of rue du Dragon. These gestures of scorn, she believed, would one day turn the tide. Lamaze admired her determination, her inability to tolerate evil. Everyone expected him to match her energy, but he seemed to be at a loss for what to do, mesmerized by the extent of the disaster.

His turning point came in February 1941. The Gestapo had just dismantled the branches of the *Musée de l'Homme,* and most of its members had been shot or deported. One evening Lamaze got a telephone call asking him to hide one who had escaped at rue du Dragon. The call revived his interest in life. From that point onward he became part of the Resistance. From Father Robert Vallery-Radot he learned the value of teamwork and the meaning of solidarity. In the course of the war, he met men like Jean Dalsace, Maurice Mayer, Paul Milliez, Auguste and Simone Gillot, all of whom after the war would be allies in his fight for his birthing method.

His Resistance work also reintroduced him to Dr. Yves Porc'her. Porc'her was a psychiatrist who in 1933 had been appointed director of the psychiatric hospitals around Paris and the suburbs. Lamaze had met him once in the 1920s and found they had much in common. For one thing, Porc'her knew everything about the Lorraine, Lamaze's home; in fact, he knew more than Lamaze did about the region. He was a member of organizations studying the area's water and climate and was especially interested in the effects mineral waters from the Vosges had on the autonomic nervous system. Lamaze had been dazzled by the range of the man's knowledge, but they had lost touch as their work took them in different directions. The war reunited them. Porc'her was writing Resistance articles in *Libération nord* under the pseudonym Capitaine Brécourt and also headed an escape network known as the Shelburn Ring. An anonymous letter led to his arrest, and he was incarcerated at Fresnes Prison. He then did something unique in the annals of the Resistance. To trick his German captors, he passed himself off as insane and simulated an aphasic ictus, which is a sudden, violent attack characterized by aphasia. His case was studied by the leading German experts in psychiatry, but his deception was difficult to detect because twenty-five years in practice had made him deeply familiar with the behavior of the mentally ill. He was subjected to the entire range of available tests. After he was taken to Beaujon Hospital for a gas encephalogram, the experts concluded that he was suffering from Alzheimer's.

After the Liberation, Porc'her calmly resumed his true identity. He was named senior medical director of Sainte-Anne Asylum and placed in charge of the Henri-Roussel Center, where he created a renowned laboratory for "social biology." Living in the sumptuous director's mansion, between Charles-Baudelaire Park and the allée Vincent-Van-Gogh, he regularly invited the Lamazes to dinners at which the asylum's inmates did the serving. These dinners normally started at ten in the evening, since Porc'her worked late and his guests, who were mostly doctors, also kept late hours. Lamaze always felt as if he were entering a fortress when he entered the asylum and paused before the hospital chapel. He and Louise and my mother would admire the beautiful Romanesque building in the half-light. Next they went to the main courtyard to look at the ornate clock tower and its campanile.

The knowledge that behind the barred windows was so much human suffering intimidated them. Sometimes, at the bend in a path, a zombielike figure would surge toward them—a patient being taken to the south wing of the hospital, where the ground-floor lights were kept on day and night. The director's mansion, located behind blue gates, seemed like a haven of peace. A statue of a suggestively supine woman sat in the front yard, which was filled with flowerbeds and illuminated by torches leading along a path to a kitchen garden. For a moment one could almost believe that, rather than located in an insane asylum, the director's house was a country estate. Still, moved by the suffering around her, Louise mistrusted the false calm of the place. She also strongly disapproved of the idea of being served dinner by inmates. However often it was explained to her that Sainte-Anne was dedicated to the principle of integrating the mentally ill back into society, she saw it as exploitation. Fernand laughed and called her oversensitive. Louise, for her part, believed that daily contact with death and suffering made doctors insensitive. She recalled that when she was working as a nurse there had been boisterous parties in the hospital staff rooms, right next door to where people were dying.

Porc'her was especially proud of two of his difficult cases. One was a man named Yves, a former butcher who had killed his wife and wounded his daughter with the tools of his trade. Now he worked in the kitchens. Then there was Micheline, a pale, shriveled old lady with trembling hands who served dinner. Porc'her saved her story for the end of the meal, when dessert was being served. With obvious relish, he would tell his guests how for thirty years Micheline believed that she was Charlotte Corday—the woman who murdered the revolutionary Marat in his bathtub—and indeed had killed her poor husband in his bathtub. Porc'her was always delighted with the effect this story had on his rapt audience.

These colorful tales interested Lamaze far less than that of a housemaid whose peculiar behavior had caught his attention. Her name was Zélie, and she was from Guadeloupe; Porc'her had been treating her for years for chronic hallucinatory psychosis. Whenever anyone rang the front doorbell, Zélie would take five minutes to answer it and always arrive looking crestfallen. After observing this a few times, Lamaze decided to spy on her through the kitchen window. He watched her while she bustled about, until suddenly the doorbell would interrupt her work. Instead of answering it immediately, she would remain standing where she was, as if in suspense, occasionally making tentative gestures of being about to move, picking objects up and then putting them back down, until finally hurrying off to answer the door. The bell caused an automatic reflex that seemed temporarily to render her scattered and confused, until finally she reacted to it normally. Zélie's case was a topic of passionate debate between Lamaze and Porc'her. Through it Lamaze deepened his understanding of Pavlov's research before witnessing its application to childbirth during his trip to Russia in 1951.

My mother regarded these visits to Sainte-Anne as you would a performance. They were in their way escapes for her; she became friends with Porc'her's wife, who was a great music lover and who sensed Anne-Marie's gift for it. Mme Porc'her quietly introduced my mother to one of her very good friends, a woman named Mme Gorjiades. Mme Gorjiades was a singing coach by profession but also a psychic who believed she had the power to alter the fate of those whom she liked. The experience proved liberating for my mother, whose voice became really superb, and who blossomed once she began to break free from the paternal bonds. Anne-Marie came into her own during this period. She even found the strength to resist her father when he tried to get her to marry a doctor whom she found sad and boring. By this point, Jean Gutmann was back in Paris after being away for twelve years; he couldn't take his eyes off this beautiful young woman whom he had sat on his knee as a child.

It was, to say the least, a very unlikely match. Jean was twenty-five years older than Anne-Marie; he had three children and a wife to whom he had been married for thirty-three years. He was entering late middle age just as Anne-Marie was entering adulthood. But love cares little for such details. And Jean was a charming man. He had a sensual mouth, handsome blue eyes, a debonair, devil-may-care attitude—he wore a cotton scarf around his neck like Gary Cooper—and beautiful and impeccably manicured nails.

Their relationship was a well-guarded secret. Louise saw to that. Fernand never suspected the liaison between his daughter and former charge, whose merit was that he was the son of his deceased best friend. "The boy can't stay in one place," Fernand would grumble as he watched this father of three rocking back and forth agitatedly in his chair. Oddly, the same man who had become such a master of adultery never saw through the thousand little lies that surrounded Jean and Anne-Marie's affair—not the afternoons upstairs in Gabrielle's room, who used the opportunity to go bargain-hunting with Louise, nor the nights spent in hotels, nor even Anne-Marie's sudden interest in Brittany, where she rented a house in Carnac, six miles from the Gutmann family home.

Blind and deaf to his surroundings, Fernand never suspected anything. Beginning in September 1951, other matters were absorbing all his attention.

PART FOUR

THE QUEST FOR UTOPIA

The imagination, that Chinese
executioner who dispenses fear
—ALAIN (EMILE CHARTIER)

In the Land of the Soviets

THE AEROFLOT PLANE containing the twelve doctors from the French delegation was preparing for takeoff. They were supposed to arrive in Moscow at 1 P.M., which would give them enough time to enjoy their caviar and champagne—the Soviets were pulling out all the stops to welcome their French guests.

His nose glued to the porthole, Lamaze pretended to be absorbed in the scenery. His colleagues' conversation bored him to tears. On the other hand, they represented a Who's Who of French medicine at the time: three professors; the celebrated pediatrician Benjamin Weill-Hallé, accompanied by his wife, a gynecologist, and by their seven-year-old daughter, who wouldn't stop running up and down the aisle; Professor Heuyer, a child psychiatrist; and Dr. Wertheimer, a surgeon from the Lyon medical school. In addition, there was Dr. Moutier, president of the French Society of Gastroenterologists, and the distinguished Dr. Bourguigon, a member of the Academy of Medicine and known for his conservative viewpoints. Next came the members of the French Communist Party: two rhinolaryngologists, Yves Cachin, an assistant physician at La Pitié Hospital, and Dr. Wicart, from the Institute of Cancer; Dr. Descamps, a tuberculosis specialist at Beaujon Hospital, and Dr. Lafitte, a psychiatrist from Saint-Antoine Hospital.

Lamaze had been a last-minute addition to the list; he had agreed to replace the director of Bluets Hospital, Pierre Rouquès, who was too ill to take the trip. The two men had known each other during the Resistance. Lamaze had hidden Rouquès in his apartment for several months during the war when the Germans were hunting him down as a militant Communist. After Liberation, Lamaze and Rouquès served together on a committee whose job it was to decide the fate of doctors who had collaborated with the Germans during the occupation. Lamaze was recognized for his impartiality and sense of justice. He prided himself on being unaffiliated and apolitical, and he intended to stay that way. Although he shared many of his Communist friends' convictions, he refused to be recruited by the Party and never carried the card.

In 1947 Rouquès invited Lamaze to join the staff at Bluets, and the offer was accepted immediately. Lamaze was made director of obstetrics for the Federation of Metal Workers, which was governed by the union called the *Confédération Générale du Travail,* or the General Confederation of Workers, under the leadership of Benoît Frachon. By having accepted the post, Lamaze was immediately pegged by his medical colleagues as a Communist. He made no attempt to either deny or confirm their assumptions. He continued to divide his career between his lucrative practice among wealthy patrons and his working-class patients at Bluets. Lamaze was now past the age of sixty and might easily have chosen to go on contentedly as he had for thirty years, resting on the laurels of his many accomplishments. He was taking an enormous risk by agreeing to go to the Soviet Union. In the early years of the Cold War one did not cross the Iron Curtain with impunity; his enemies would not forgive him for it.

Their Soviet hosts were waiting at the Moscow airport to take the

French doctors to the National Hotel, located next to Red Square. As soon as he got to his room, Lamaze collapsed onto his bed, exhausted and suffering from a migraine. He felt completely disoriented. In his mind, Russia was supposed to be snow-covered, a glittering empire of frost, and yet the temperature had reached 104 degrees in the shade. The place was an inferno. Disoriented or not, however, Lamaze came to the Soviet Union with his eyes open. He was not fooled by the massive propaganda campaign associated with this trip, whose purpose was to convince the forty-eight delegations from around the world, including the French doctors, of the great progress made by Soviet medicine. For a month the foreigners were stuffed with caviar and pretty speeches. They visited scores of laboratories, hospitals, and maternity wards, each one freshly painted and spruced up.

The hotel room was small but comfortable and had a radio and a safe. Dingy yellow wallpaper was blistering in places from the humidity. Lamaze wanted to get up and drink a glass of water, but his migraine seemed to keep him from moving. There was one element about this trip about which he was very excited, and that was the opportunity to witness firsthand the new method of childbirth being employed by Russian obstetricians, and based on Pavlov's theories. He had heard Professor A. Nicolaïev from Leningrad present his research about this method at the International Congress of Gynecology in Paris the previous June; what he learned had done far more than pique his curiosity. The whole notion that you could help a woman reduce pain from uterine contractions without chemical inducement was deeply exciting. He had been thinking about the method constantly. And now he would have the chance to see it at work with his own eyes. He had vowed he would not leave the Soviet Union until he seen and learned everything he could.

The first two weeks of the visit went as Lamaze expected they would—tightly controlled and monitored by the Russian authorities.

Supervised by Dr. Pankine, Professor Denissov, and Professor Lebedeva, a former nurse who was now a lung specialist, the French doctors traveled around Moscow and its suburbs. Each step went according to a plan: the children's gardens, the library of the Medical Institute, the Tretiakov Museum, the Krasny Proletari factory, the walks on the dock of the Moscow River. Their visit to Botkine Hospital lasted five hours, the one to Clara Zetkin Maternity Hospital in the Molotov district took an entire day. But Lamaze still had not witnessed a single painless childbirth. He was beginning to grow impatient. He was promised that he would be given a demonstration at the end of the week.

At the end of these two weeks, Comrade Smirnov, the Soviet minister of public health, met with the French doctors and launched into an enthusiastic speech about the Soviet medical system and how it was working in each of the country's sixteen republics. Medical care in the Soviet Union, he announced, was free, and dispensed by 250,000 doctors—as compared with the 25,000 doctors who had practiced under the czars. Every single district boasted a clinic with a large staff of doctors in every discipline and field. The life of the Soviet doctor should be the envy of the West, Smirnov told them, for they started out on a fixed salary that would increase according to seniority and merit, and their shifts were limited to six hours per day, allowing them plenty of time for research.

The meeting ended late in the evening, at which point the guests, drunk on vodka and stuffed with caviar, stumbled off to the French embassy, where a midnight banquet was planned in their honor. They were in high spirits. Even the normally dour Pankine was tipsy and flirting with the delegation's interpreter, Sofia. Lamaze, on the other hand, was foaming with rage. His visit to Professor Petrov had been cancelled yet again; he would have to wait until they returned to

Leningrad to get any chance of seeing the new childbirth technique at work. He was beginning to think the whole thing was a hoax.

Suddenly he made up his mind to go off by himself. It was now or never. Lowering his head, Lamaze ducked into a crowd of people heading for downtown Moscow. When he got to Pushkin Square, he merged with a group of boisterous students heading toward a café on Gorky Street. He thought he could feel Comrade Pankine's eyes glaring at him, so he picked up his pace and walked for almost an hour along streets with buildings whose facades were brilliantly illuminated, following the flow of the pedestrians. When he came to the building that housed *Isvesztia,* the Soviet newspaper, he stopped, out of breath. Midnight had just struck. He looked around and found that he seemed to be on his own. At a wooden kiosk that sold smoked herring and draft beer he celebrated his newfound freedom.

Night made the city seem mysterious and strange. Lamaze wandered aimlessly, looking at faces. Most seemed ravaged by alcohol, and none conformed to the images he had concocted of Russians from all those great novels. He began following a tall, thin man, whose outline vaguely reminded him of a character out of a Gogol story, but the man strode away, disappearing into Red Square. In front of the GUM department store, a patrol of Communist Youth Leaguers went by, dragging off the last drunks. A trolley was getting ready to leave; unthinkingly, Lamaze jumped onto it. Drowsy from the mix of beer and vodka, he rode through a run-down neighborhood in which the older houses were in the process of being razed by bulldozers. Then he found himself at the terminus, on a street pitted with holes and ruts. A fetid smell came from the small courtyards of half-gutted houses inside which lived entire families. Hardly anyone was still on the street—aside from a few drunks sleeping it off under some garbage, and the occasional prostitute on the prowl for a last client. One prostitute approached him. For a moment she reminded him of Sofia, the delegation's attractive interpreter—those large dark eyes in which you could get lost. But he was too old, and she reeked of wine. He pulled away from her. The adventure was over; it was time to return to the hotel and rejoin the others on the paths carefully marked out by their Soviet hosts.

The delegation left the next morning for Georgia. Quietly and diplomatically, Yves Cachin had taken control as leader of the French delegation. Hiding behind his pipe smoke, his sharp eyes missed nothing, and he noted every weakness. His being the head of the delegation earned him the favors of Sofia, pushing aside poor Pankine. Pankine consoled himself by swilling *tchatcha,* the local alcohol, and stuffing himself with giant pickles—he always had a store of them stuffed in a blue-checked napkin, which had taken on legendary status among the delegation. After he had finished the last one, his tongue would loosen and he would tell anyone who would listen about his hopes and dreams, which were essentially those of your average petty, zealous apparatchik. There was the car he hoped to buy after three years on a waiting list, the scams he was organizing with some bigwig from the Commission of Apartments.

The weather continued to be stiflingly hot. After being treated to a tour of the Joseph Stalin Museum in the city of Gorky, the delegation was taken to the hills of Tbilisi where, all in one day, they visited a maternity hospital, went to a fair, and toured monasteries in which lived Armenian monks in long black cassocks. Exhausted from the heat and the pace, Lamaze didn't even have the energy to complain. After three weeks of rosy speeches and hearty handshakes with officials, he had resigned himself to the fact that he would leave the country without witnessing the new childbirth technique. Then, however, he had a meeting that changed everything.

Hidden in a birch wood at the edge of a river, the Marx Maternity Hospital had a total of eight beds—not counting the three in the delivery room—and served three hundred denizens of four farm collectives. At the head of the hospital's staff, composed of two midwives and an obstetrician, was a doctor named Linkov, a man of about forty. He welcomed Lamaze warmly and in nearly flawless French told him about the work he had been doing for the past ten years to perfect the psychoprophylactic method. This method, Linkov told him, was based on the psychic and physical preparation of the pregnant woman and required no medication. The whole idea was extremely practical, consisting of breathing exercises that permitted the woman to remain a conscious participant in each phase of childbirth. During those ten years, Linkov announced proudly, there had been not one single case of either maternal or infant mortality.

To a seasoned practitioner like Lamaze, what Linkov was telling him seemed highly unlikely. But his curiosity had the better of him, and he listened attentively while Linkov lectured him about the theoretical foundations of his research. The Pavlovian school had demonstrated the cortical nature of pain sensation. Starting in 1912, following up on work started in Pavlov's laboratory, Professor Erofeeva started working on the conditioned transformation of pain and had proved that pain could be suppressed through the intervention of other conditioning. The eminent Dr. I. Velvoski decided to apply Pavlov's work to the psychoprophylaxis of pain: to condition pain responses by using the stronger stimulus of language, and to trigger pain-blocking reflexes in pregnant women. The method had spread throughout Russia. Accordingly, the women at the Marx farm collective were given training sessions at the hospital, beginning in the first months of pregnancy; they were also given booklets that demonstrated how to continue the training in their homes.

Lamaze was impressed. If everything Linkov said was true, this man was a miracle worker. After his talk, Linkov took Lamaze into a darkened room where four women were waiting for their checkup. He asked one of the women to follow them into his office. A young peasant woman stood up with difficulty, the size of her belly indicating that she was nearing the end of her pregnancy. She seemed quite at ease about being in the clinic and preceded them into the room, where without any embarrassment she took her clothes off and lay down on the examining table. From an iron box, Dr. Linkov removed a long needle and walked toward her, speaking quickly in Russian. The young woman began to roll her eyes. Her features contracted, and instinctively she pulled her hand away the moment the needle came near it. The doctor burst out laughing, and patted her shoulder while continuing to speak. The young woman responded with a large smile. Linkov then turned to Lamaze:

"I've just explained to this first-time mother-to-be what the pain of childbirth really is: an old wives' tales. I've pointed out to her that if I had pricked her with this needle, she would in fact have suffered because she would have dreaded the pain. But look at her hands, how they're all covered with prick wounds from her sewing. When she pricks herself while stitching something, she feels nothing, or almost nothing. The pains of childbirth are essentially the same."

The young woman was somewhat disconcerted that these two men were discussing her in a language she couldn't understand. At the end of the day, Linkov escorted Lamaze to the exit, then gave him a dozen or so brochures on the psychoprophylactic method. They were written, of course, in Russian. Lamaze thanked him, but thought that, being unable to decipher their meaning, he would probably simply throw them away.

Some of Lamaze's doubts were allayed, though he suspected that what Linkov was telling him was propaganda. The Soviet doctor had given a convincing performance. Still, the question remained whether the technique could be universalized or was peculiar to Russia, a country that historically had placed great faith in the power of shamans and healers. The legendary French explorer Gérard de Nerval once wrote during one of his trips to Asia that he was too "skeptical to reject any superstition." Lamaze left the hospital understanding what Nerval had meant. He needed more proof.

The end of Lamaze's stay at Leningrad went badly. Time and again he was promised that he would be allowed to visit a pioneer hospital and witness a birth using the new method, and time and again he was disappointed. Lamaze withdrew into a more and more worrisome silence. Forty-eight hours before he was supposed to leave, they told him that Dr. Nicolaïev had left for Kiev and that their meeting would have to be postponed. Lamaze exploded. He demanded to see a childbirth immediately, threatening that if he didn't he would denounce them to the international press as frauds. Finally, on September 4, 1951, while visiting the Pavlov Institute in Koltouchi, he was informed that Nicolaïev was returning from Kiev and that Lamaze would be permitted to witness a woman having painless childbirth.

He did indeed witness the procedure, and while there are no records of his immediate reactions, we have what he told the newspaper *Libération* after his return to France. "Pain may seem to be the inevitable ransom of childbirth, but it isn't any longer," he said.

I saw with my own eyes a woman give birth without pain. I witnessed it. I've been in obstetric practice for thirty years. I couldn't have been fooled. Painless childbirth's success, without any other treatment or the use of drugs, is almost unbelievable. . . . The method has spread throughout the Soviet Union . . . and it should be used in all the countries of the world.

Many cried fraud. Some said Lamaze had been duped. But by this point such accusations mattered little. A new technique had been proposed, and the taboo subject of childbirth pain was now open for discussion. A new way of thinking was being born.

Bluets

THE LECTURE WAS TO TAKE PLACE at 3 P.M. at the Claude-Bernard Medical Center. That morning Lamaze had taken advantage of a moment's respite to come to the hospital to rest. As soon as he sat down at his desk and put his head on his arms, he sank into a deep sleep, interrupted by the chief supervisor, as he had instructed, at 2 P.M. sharp.

The moment had come to present the public with nearly two years of results on the application of the psychoprophylactic method in France. During this time, five hundred deliveries had been performed at Bluets with a 92 percent success rate. Moreover, the number of cesarians had declined dramatically, women were getting out of bed sooner, and there were fewer cases of phlebitis, because the duration of labor had shortened.

Who would have been able to predict such stunning results in September 1951 when, on the same day he returned from Russia, Lamaze summoned the entire maternity staff into his office and, his voice filled with emotion, told them about what had happened? An ancient curse had been lifted. A new kind of childbirth was at hand, and it was free of risk for both mother and child. Rather than drugs, it was based upon coaching, which began three months before the due date.

His announcement was greeted with astonishment. Every member of the staff remained uncomfortably silent, not wanting to hurt Lamaze's feelings with their skepticism. "Now we'll have to grit our teeth whenever we think about the spiritual father of the people," one midwife dared utter. But over the course of the next few hours, and late into the evening, the staff's reservations began to melt away before the intensity of Lamaze's conviction. His enthusiasm was contagious. And most important, he was considered one of the wisest, least political, and most levelheaded of physicians. Soon they had overcome their disbelief—or at least had accepted that the hypothesis he was advancing was worth putting to test. They agreed to start work immediately.

Bluets Hospital was a former warehouse for machine tools, located on rue des Bluets, in the eleventh arrondissement of Paris. The hospital was one of many institutions run by the Federation of Metal Workers of the Seine, one of France's largest unions. The other organizations run by the union included professional night schools, rest homes, resorts, and flying clubs. Yet it was this small hospital that was to become a Cold War battlefield, the locus of one of the era's bitterest and strangest political confrontations.

Under Lamaze's direction, doctors and midwives were trained in the new technique and immersed in the works of Pavlov and Velvoski; that training proceeded slowly and was based upon empirical processes. All the nonmedical personnel, from the cleaning lady to the switchboard operator, were mobilized as well. Lamaze was keenly aware that even one small misstep in the treatment of patients could endanger the whole mission behind his method. The hospital was remodeled—walls were demolished to create large conference rooms to which pregnant women could come for training sessions. The delivery rooms were divided up to separate patients during childbirth. A pediatrics clinic was opened on the ground floor; here doctors and nurses could talk to patients and instruct them in the rudiments of newborn care. With fifty-two beds that could accommodate roughly two hundred women per month, Bluets was transformed into a veritable research laboratory.

Lamaze worked tirelessly, constantly experimenting with new techniques. The essence of his research involved changing the conditions in which phenomena occurred in order to alter the phenomena themselves. His first goal was to make the psychoprophylactic method universal. After that he began refining it, adapting it to French habits and tastes, and in the process distancing himself from the Pavlovian idea that humans were merely "conditionable" flesh and bones. He experimented with various relaxation techniques, such as using the "small dog" panting method—short, sharp breaths rather than deep respiration. Lamaze also believed that the father ought to be brought into the labor room; his presence was an integral part of the birth process. By itself, that one simple change in procedure became a powerful force for creating equality among couples. Expectant fathers were also encouraged to attend the preparatory course, which was taught by an obstetrician and midwives. Aided by her spouse and by the medical team, the woman became an active player; the foundation of the Lamaze Method was that women should be empowered to deliver their own children. Unlike the Russians, Lamaze made his method available to all women, regardless of how their fetuses were positioned in the womb. After long months of trial and error, he finally succeeded in shaping his own version of the Russian method. It employed rigor but was free of doctrinal rigidity; and it belonged to women everywhere.

In February 1952 Madeleine Tsouladzé became the first woman in France to give birth using the Lamaze Method. Though the birth was difficult and the baby was in the breech position, she did not seem to have suffered at all from pain. Lamaze let his student Pierre Vellay and physician's assistant Blanche Cohen perform the delivery—a symbolic gesture signifying his hope that his method would continue after he was gone. Almost immediately, the news that you didn't have to suffer to have a baby spread like wildfire. Women by the hundreds were requesting to have their babies delivered at Bluets.

Now, as he was preparing for his lecture at the Claude-Bernard Clinic, Lamaze was focusing on the second stage of his grand project: convincing the French government to allocate funds for training doctors and midwives in maternity hospitals throughout the entire country. He knew that the reaction he got to his lecture that afternoon would be a decisive factor in whether or not he succeeded.

Lamaze's stomach was in knots. He used the pretext of a forgotten folder, a light that hadn't been turned off, to put off leaving the hospital for the lecture hall. He was a man of the clinical world, uncomfortable with the public arena. But there was no turning back now. The fight was on. Most of his wealthy clientele had abandoned him when he took the job at Bluets; most of his former colleagues were convinced he had lost his mind—one had even spit in his face while passing him in the street. He had dared to believe Soviet propaganda, and he had dared to defy biblical injunction. And if that were not already enough to earn him enemies, he was proposing a system that reduced the need for surgical interventions such as cesarians, thereby taking money from his colleagues' pockets. The Medical Board, the colossal and self-regulating bureaucratic machine that governed the health of French citizens, was preparing to mount an attack against him.

It was time to leave. Lamaze slowly walked down the stairs, giving a mock salute to the portrait of Stalin hanging in the Bluet's entrance hall.

Irène, his chauffeur, was waiting for him in the car, smoking nervously. Now his chauffeur and secretary, she had also once been his mistress. Irène was a formidable woman who believed in order; she couldn't bear the slightest deviation from schedule. Angry that he was late, she waited for him to close the door, then did a high-speed U-turn, the tires screeching. Lamaze gripped the armrest. On the backseat were a bundle of letters she had brought him from home.

He thumbed distractedly through the usual slanderous letters that arrived in a flood each morning, filled with adjectives and epithets: "heathen," "sinner," "fiend," "murderer," and, worst of all, "Communist." He noted that the more vicious ones lacked any sort of stylistic grace and were mired in clichés. Fortunately, here and there were letters containing expressions of gratitude that cheered him.

The car was passing by the Pantheon when he opened a small vellum envelope. It was a brief note from Laure Duval. As usual, it was filled with grammatical mistakes and solecisms. Mixing in English words she thought made her insipid prose chic, Laure wrote that she was covering him with kisses. Not satisfied with drowning him in saccharine verbiage, she had included a photograph, showing them sitting at a table, their arms around each other: "In memory of that unforgettable day," she had written. Lamaze took out a pen and blocked out her face with black ink.

Trompe l'oeil

HOW DIFFICULT IT WAS to understand the prudish, moralistic side of a man who openly practiced polygamy and adultery. The issue was systematically avoided by the people with whom I talked about my grandfather. One woman, however, spoke about it in a quite open but nonjudgmental fashion, helping me to clarify one of the many contradictions of the "good Dr. Lamaze."

I got in touch with Marie-Jeanne Detoeuf on the advice of Jacques Caron. An hour after calling her, I found myself sitting in her apartment, where she welcomed me with charming simplicity and then immediately launched into the subject of Lamaze. Her apartment, she explained, had belonged originally to her father-in-law, Auguste Detoeuf, and it was here that she first met Lamaze. His large, sad eyes had made a strong impression on her. He seemed so out of place in a society salon, mixing with the barons of the press and their spiteful spouses. That Auguste had chosen Lamaze as a friend did not surprise her; her father-in-law detested those snobs whose company was forced upon him by his wife. They met during a 1927 conference organized by the Annales circle—the preeminent group of historians of that time, so called because their method involved sifting of everyday sources, rather than focussing on "great events"—and they hit it off immediately. Their shared interest in history created a bond that would last until Auguste's death in 1947. Lamaze had continued to frequent the Detoeuf circle even after his friend's death. I wondered what induced him to keep attending these salons—whether it was from habit or some form of masochism. He had almost nothing in common with the kinds of people who went to Detoeuf's, a Who's Who of Paris media figures, particularly those with right-wing tendencies. Leading the pack was Pierre Brisson, editor of the conservative *Le Figaro* newspaper, who along with his sister Françoise dominated discussions. They tolerated Lamaze—without Louise, of course—only because of his intellectual interests and his wit. Lamaze seemed to be a kind of circus bear at the gatherings, willing to do tricks for a lump of sugar. One favorite after-dinner pastime was testing Lamaze's memory, asking him to recite entire verses from *The Legend of the Centuries* or from *Athalie*. He played the part beautifully, unafraid of or impervious to their mockery, seemingly content to show off and entertain them. The lump of sugar, in this case, was Laure Duval, a regular at the Detoeuf salon. The feelings she had aroused in Fernand were both preposterous and overpowering, and damaging as well.

"Laure Legron—that was Duval's married name—felt nothing for him, unless it was contempt with a slight tinge of tenderness," added Mme Detoeuf. "When her husband died, she found Lamaze panting at her side, as enamored as he was gullible. He was so patiently insistent that eventually she gave in. Their relationship was stormy, of course. After it had ended, Laure kept him around and used him badly. Fernand didn't mind: 'Be a sucker and be proud of it,' he used to say. But it was pure facade. Beneath his Herculean exterior he knew he was weak because he was vulnerable. He would have loved to have been the vanquishing conquerer, armored in self-confidence.

But doubt gnawed at him, and the pettiness of those who attacked him drained his courage. He naively placed his trust in human nature, and when he was attacked he tried to defend himself, but each new blow took something out of him. Without Louise, he would never have taken up the battle for painless childbirth."

Mme Detoeuf stopped, lit a cigarette, then showed me a photo showing her holding a chubby baby in her arms.

"That's Benoît, my third child. He was an accident. When I was helping Lamaze in 1951 during his first lectures on his method, I was pregnant with Benoît without knowing it. Your grandfather looked me straight in the eye and said, 'Come back in nine months.' I was dumbfounded. A week later, I learned that I was pregnant.

"I've never met a better diagnostician. He had an astonishing clinical acuity that put him miles ahead of his colleagues, even those who had more diplomas on their walls. The value of that acuity has been lost now. Scanners are replacing sound medical judgment, and doctors hide behind their answering machines. Lamaze never took vacations. He was wholeheartedly dedicated to every one of his patients. They were his life. When he understood that he could no longer practice the way he wanted to, it killed him."

"What are you saying?" I interrupted, taken aback.

"I don't know very much," Mme Detoeuf answered, with a gentle smile. "On a Tuesday—March fifth—your grandfather returned home from a stormy meeting at Bluets. He called me that night, sobbing. The Metal Workers' union was claiming that it had to stop supporting his birthing method, supposedly because of a management problem at the hospital. That seemed very strange, since doctors from all over the world were hurrying to Bluets to learn the Lamaze technique.

"They threw him out like a thief. He was so crushed that he couldn't even finish his sentences. I knew he would never recover from an affront like that. The next morning he was found dead of a heart attack.

"I can't really take sides. Other people can tell you more about what was behind it all. But those secrets are well guarded, especially after forty years of silence. The only advice I can give you is to go visit the House of Glass."

The House of Glass

I HAD BEEN PUTTING OFF this moment for a long time, skirting the edges of the issue rather than plunging directly into the heart of it. Though I knew that at some point I would have to confront the man who might explain what happened at Bluets, I kept postponing it. It meant getting into the politics of the Lamaze Method and the whole "psychoprophylactic method," and entering into a debate I found daunting. I was not sure I was up for playing the role of militant defender. The man in question was Lamaze's former colleague and student Pierre Vellay.

The silence surrounding Lamaze's work in France today seems profoundly unjust to me. When I was twelve I heard my grandfather's name and memory being maligned on one of France's biggest radio stations. I rushed over to the studio. I found Vellay already there, having a heated on-air discussion with the author of a satirical tract entitled *Les Bateleurs du mal joli (Snake Oil Salesmen),* in which the Lamaze Method was derided as pure charlatanism. The method was in decline in those days, mainly because of lack of money and conviction. Filled with youthful rage, I waited at the exit for the author, whose name was Marie-Josée Jaubert, to come out so that I could scream insults at her. She did, and I did. The poor woman gaped at me in total silence. So did Vellay. My feeling of vindication faded with time. Though my grandfather's name was slowly being relegated to the history books, his memory continued to gnaw at me. I felt like his coconspirator. Jean-Paul Sartre tells us that not taking sides means joining the other side, and in this case the other side consisted of people determined to erase Lamaze's contributions.

Before meeting with Vellay again I went over what I needed to discuss with him: Lamaze's two trips to the Soviet Union, his trial before the Medical Board, and the mystery of his death in 1957. But everything was a blur in my head: the names of the Russian scientists—Erofeeva, Pavlov, Bykov, and Nikolaïev; the functioning of the central nervous system and the theories of conditioned reflexes; the "Doctor's Plot" of 1953, when fifteen doctors, most of them Jewish, were accused of plotting to kill Soviet officials; and the Soviet invasion of Hungary. While waiting to go in to meet Vellay, I paced up and down the sidewalk in front of his building, past the ediface housing the famous Institute of Political Sciences, reviewing in my mind my recent readings of works by Lamaze and his colleagues—the numberless books and articles on obstetrics, midwifery, maternity hospitals, and parenting. I didn't know what from this enormous collection of documentation I would need to draw upon. Perhaps, I worried, it had all been a way of protecting myself, and my grandfather.

I stopped in front of the door to Vellay's apartment building, not yet ready to go inside. Suddenly the door opened and a stooped old lady came out, pulled by a black poodle on a leash.

"Alexandre, would you wait for me, please," she said to her pet irritably.

This made me smile. Anywhere dogs were named Alexandre couldn't be that intimidating. I opened the door and walked toward the House of Glass.

Built by the famous architect Pierre Charrot in 1928 for the wealthy Dalsace family, the House of Glass has long been an object of fascination and mystery. Constructed between the courtyard and the garden of an existing apartment house, its mystery lies in the fact that you cannot see it from the street. You open the outer door, and suddenly there it is straight in front you, a colossus of glass and steel through which the light pours, giving the impression that nothing separates the inside from the outside. Creating that illusion was one of the principles upon which the building was constructed. Because you can see the screws and joists that hold it together, your first thought is that everything is visible. And then you begin to realize that such transparency is deceptive.

I was met by Vellay's secretary, who led me into an immense space that served as the living room. The doctor was late, she told me, and sent his apologies. I sat down on a black art deco couch, which was the only furniture in the room aside from some movable bookcases. I realized that the interior to the building consisted of a system of sliding parts: doors and panels, trompe-l'oeil openings, retractable staircases. The midday sun was streaming through the glass roof, yet, perhaps because of all the metal, the luminosity felt cold. After an hour of waiting, I began to wonder whether Dr. Vellay had forgotten our meeting.

I heard the sound of footsteps. The secretary appeared and asked me to follow her. She led me through a maze of passageways. If I had tried to find my way on my own I would have instantly lost my bearings. A door opened and I entered Vellay's office.

The room looked out on an overgrown garden and was filled with curios—African masks, photos of children—that clashed with the austerity of the decor; in contrast to the sterility of the surroundings they seemed dreamlike, invitations to a distant landscape. Vellay approached me, smiling. His eyes also bespoke memories of distant times and faraway places. He graciously requested I sit down and then asked me to give him a few more minutes. He had one last thing to tend to before we spoke.

While he looked through a thick file, I quietly observed this former student of my grandfather's. His thick gray hair gave the impression that he was younger than his seventy years. He must have charmed quite a few people with his calm, casual manner. Suddenly he looked up at me.

"So, let's get down to it. What do you want from me?"

I could not speak. I thought for a second that he had forgotten I was Lamaze's granddaughter. I had made a point of sending him a detailed letter about my work, and had called his assistant the day before to confirm our meeting. A flood of confused thoughts engulfed me. I debated whether I should simply get up, apologize, and leave. It was obvious that Vellay was amused by my confusion. He was smiling.

"Don't worry. Jacques Caron told me about your research. But I don't know if I can be of much help. Even so, I've written something for you. It's my attempt to sum up the high points of the struggle Lamaze and I were involved in. Memory plays tricks on you at my age. I'm no longer sure of dates, and my wife, who could provide some of the details, is unfortunately not here today."

Dr. Vellay seized the file in front of him—the same file he had been perusing a few moments earlier—and pulled out a sheaf of pages. He seemed hesitant, as if struggling to find the right words to tell the story of what had happened more than forty years earlier. He cleared his throat. His hands were shaking. Then he began:

"I met your grandfather for the first time at Bluets. It was in 1947. I was twenty-eight. As he walked toward me, I thought I was looking at the statue of the Commandatore from Mozart's *Don Giovanni* come to life. I couldn't speak; I was literally petrified. Then he started to talk to me in a gentle voice that didn't at all match his intimidating demeanor. He said some kind things, and my fear quickly receded. We talked for quite a long time. I felt we were on the same wavelength. When I left him I felt wide awake, as if I'd become more intelligent simply through contact with him. Later I learned that honest men have a talent for making things seem better; Lamaze was an honest man in the fullest sense of the term.

"I often saw him on the subway but didn't dare say hello for fear of interrupting his reading. He was always reading. Every morning you'd see him, walking in slow, deliberate steps toward the hospital, a book in his hand, never appearing to be in a hurry despite the crushing mound of work waiting for him.

"My father-in-law, Jean Dalsace, was actually the one who brought Lamaze and me together. Dalsace was a great figure in the Resistance, a leader among the Communist intelligentsia. He was also one of the pioneers of women's liberation. In 1936 he began leading the fight for contraception. He deeply appreciated Lamaze's free spirit. When Pierre Rouquès appointed your grandfather to be head of obstetrics at Bluets, Dalsace suggested he take me on as assistant."

Vellay stopped to light a cigarette and then went back to his story. In great detail he told the saga of the beginnings of the Lamaze Method at Bluets. Remembering that exciting period seemed to cheer him up. We laughed together about what it was that made Lamaze sometimes seem like a good little schoolboy. He touched on the voyage to Russia in less detail but told me that he hoped his wife, Aline, might have saved the notes taken by Lamaze during his visit.

We had been talking for over an hour, moving from subject to subject, when suddenly Vellay's face clouded over:

"Let us move on to serious subjects. Now I'm going to have to reveal to you how base the human soul can be. After the joy of creation comes the pettiness of politics."

He lit a second cigarette.

"In the Soviet Union, the psychoprophylactic method had become standard practice very soon after it had been proposed. It seemed like the answer to a national problem. Lamaze asked the French government to do the same: to teach the psychoprophylactic method to all doctors in every hospital. He fought for what was right, without for a second suspecting what sort of forces he was unleashing.

"Our big mistake was going directly to the public, without passing through the official channels. Actually, Lamaze considered women to be his best spokespeople, and instead of first publishing his findings in *The Hospital Weekly,* as he should have, he gave a public lecture at the Claude-Bernard Medical Center. The second lecture took place in May 1953, before the entire scientific community. Lamaze played a film that for the first time showed the complete course of a painless childbirth. The popular press took the story and made it into front-page material. Reporters told their readers that they were overcome by a birth in which the only cry was that of the newborn child. Columnists took the government to task with one ceaseless argument: instead of spending millions on the war in Indochina, why weren't they helping Dr. Lamaze develop his method so that French women could give birth without pain? In May 1954, the national radio station played a spectacular broadcast—a recording of a birth using the Lamaze Method. In February 1955, Francis Crémieux's recording of *Painless Childbirth* was released and became one of the best-selling records of the year. Several months later, Lamaze published the book that would become the bible for generations of women, *What Is Painless Childbirth?*

"All the media attention heaped on Lamaze rankled the medical authorities, who began to launch their own poisonous counteroffensive. At the Academy of Medicine, Professor Lantuéjoul challenged the whole idea of the Lamaze Method, which he argued was based on the subjective impressions of women who had been instructed in how to give birth. Twice in 1953 we were brought before the Medical Board and accused of engaging in 'false advertising.' My wife has kept the proceedings of the trial and can give you a copy if you want. Or else you can write to the headquarters of the Medical Board, although they don't like to take out their files.'"

Vellay crushed out his cigarette. His voice was now tinged with anger and bitterness.

"Despite the threats, nothing could deter us. Lamaze was infuriated by the pettiness of the attacks against him, so he decided to go against his own nature and head out into the arena. Like a pilgrim with his walking staff, he traveled to every part of the country, trying to convince doctors and administrative authorities, city by city. Some of his lectures took place in front of no more than two or three people. The taboos were difficult to overcome, but gradually he began to succeed. Starting in 1953, newspapers that were aligned with the Communist Party, *French Women* and *The Time Has Come* [*Heures claires*], launched a campaign to get the necessary funds. Each week they published interviews with mothers who had given birth without pain. These testimonies began accumulating at such a rate that women had to sign up at the tiny number of maternity hospitals that practiced the Lamaze Method before they even got pregnant.

"Faced with such overwhelming support on the part of French mothers, our enemies began to give in. Left-wing Christians were the first to rally to our side. *The Biweekly* [*La Quinzaine*], a magazine launched by the Dominicans, started a campaign in favor of the Lamaze Method, and so did *Christian Witness* [*Témoignage chrétien*]. Increasingly, doctors who had been initially skeptical were now beginning to admit the method was proving successful, and they began to join the movement. The head of Welfare Services, Dr. Leclainche, went out on a limb to plead the cause of the Lamaze Method before the Municipal Council. Devraigne publicly argued that the scientific value of the Lamaze Method outweighed its political connotations. In 1954 the Medical Board cleared us of all charges. That same year, the Municipal Council unanimously voted to allocate funds for training in the Lamaze Method, and in 1955 that funding was extended to all the maternity hospitals in France. Lamaze had made so many new changes in the Russian psychoprophylactic method that when he returned to the Soviet Union in March 1955, he was asked to present the method to doctors from around the world, most of whom had come specifically to hear him. Then the final holdouts surrendered. On January 8, 1956, before seven hundred gynecologists from all over the world who were meeting at the Vatican, Pope Pius XII gave his full and complete approval to the technique of painless childbirth, declaring that the Lamaze Method was not in itself open to moral criticism and did not contradict the words of Scripture.

"It was a veritable landslide. In 1957 the Lamaze Method was adopted in more than fifty countries, including America and China. That same year, your grandfather, who aside from his trips to Russia had never left France, was invited to Italy, Portugal, and Cuba. Doctors of every nationality came to Bluets for training, and especially to meet Lamaze. Your grandfather's gamble had paid off. He'd succeeded in broadcasting 'his truth' on an international level, from little Bluets. That was the moment they chose to get rid of him for being too old."

Drawing anxiously on a half-extinguished cigarette, Vellay seemed vexed. I was afraid to ask why and kept silent. Suddenly he looked me straight in the eyes:

"Lamaze was killed in the most cowardly way—by having discredit heaped on him. They began using gossip and innuendo. They said he had gotten too old. They wondered why he kept delivering the babies of rich women at Belvédère. They said that his private life harmed his practice at Bluets. And finally, they asked how you could trust a man who both wasn't a card-carrying member of the Communist Party and who had refused to sign a petition condemning the members of the 'Doctor's Plot' in the Soviet Union.

"After having appropriated Lamaze's work with so much fanfare, his good friends now tried to minimize its importance. 'The Lamaze Method isn't orthodox,' they said. 'It has moved too far away from the great Pavlov.' Sanctimonious lies that suppressed the truth. The truth was that the Lamaze Method was expensive and required a lot of personnel. Try to understand me, since you come from the generation living with dehumanized hospitals dominated by technological inflation. For a woman to truly benefit from the Lamaze Method, she has to be followed regularly during her pregnancy; then, during the entire period of labor, her midwife, her doctor, and a nurse have to be present. For technocrats, that's a budgetary disaster. Yes, of course, the epidural is more economical, but is stopping pain all that needs to be done in order to stop anxiety?

"So first they chipped away at the funding. Then they went through all our accounts with a fine-toothed comb, trimming the expenses, eliminating the positions one by one, the 'minor personnel,' as they called them.

"These dirty tricks really got to Lamaze. After having fought against the conformism of the medical world, here he was being betrayed by his own supposed allies, stifled by a limited, sectarian administration. Without realizing it, he'd been pushed into a political battle and had taken on the dimensions of a national figure, but his deeply idealistic nature couldn't abide such conflict. It was a game he knew he would lose.

"Sensing that there was a plot against him, he wrote out his professional last will and testament in the form of a letter, requesting that I be named to succeed him as head physician. All traces of that letter disappeared when he died.

"The last step before the end was the dismissal of the hospital's financial director. It was known that he had been Lamaze's principal supporter, and that by toppling him they were delivering a mortal blow to the man they really wanted to fire. Then they concocted a file that was made to order for their purposes—the so-called Lunet File—jammed with figures and complicated calculations, with a man's head thrown in.

"On the evening of March 5, 1957, Lamaze was called into a meeting with the Metal Workers. This was a pure formality. The decision had already been made to order a restructuring of the hospital staff and to dismiss most of his closest colleagues, actions intended to limit his activities. At the end of this very stormy meeting, Lamaze was stricken with a syncope, or fainting fit. He died from a heart attack the next morning. His death had arrived in the nick of time. The Party appreciated it and gave him a sumptuous funeral.

"There is more to tell, but I think I've said enough. You see how talkative you get with age."

Vellay got up, letting me know that it was time to go. This voyage into the past seemed to have exhausted him. Lost in thought, he led me through the maze of hallways. I didn't know how to thank him— and didn't dare raise the issue of those infamous documents he had mentioned that his wife had. He said good-bye in the living room, letting the secretary show me to the door. The House of Glass was full of secret compartments. Its door closed on new enigmas.

Wednesday, March 6, 1957

FERNAND LAMAZE LEFT THE DELIVERY ROOM with bloody hands. His fingers were long and a bit thick—clumsy-looking when they weren't practicing medicine. Throughout his career he had cared for them the way a musician does his instrument. What would he do with them now?

By 7 A.M. the hospital on rue des Bluets was beginning to fill up. At the entrance a few nervous fathers paced while their wives sat on benches, their stomachs swollen and their eyes slightly sunken, waiting for their preparatory lessons. The lunar faces of pregnant women had always fascinated Lamaze. With expressions that seemed turned inward and shapes as convex as perfect circles, they seemed from another planet. Nothing could touch them now: that other life growing in them was reaching beyond them, cutting them off from this world. Lamaze was never so happy as when delivering a baby, joining in that moment of truth when existence was unveiled, and in an experience to which a woman gave herself up totally. Ceasing to be an obstetrician would make life lose all of its meaning for him.

Mechanically he turned off the desk lamp, then put on his hat. With slumped shoulders he walked for the last time past the portrait of Benoît Frachon hanging in the lobby. How many children had he brought into this world? About two a day, including Sundays and holidays, for thirty-seven years.

At the hospital exit, Lamaze ran into one of the staff midwives, who greeted him respectfully. Lamaze was a charismatic man; he had a quiet authority that he had always known how to use. Conflict, on the other hand, took him out of his depth. And this time he lacked the courage to fight.

A gray car waited for him on the street. Irène, his chauffeur for the last ten years, sat in the driver's seat, a cigarette dangling out of the corner of her mouth, her cap pulled on sideways. Lamaze had met her right after she got out of prison in Poitiers, where she had served three years for theft and dealing in stolen property. Many wondered why Irène was so attached to the doctor. Her desire to make him happy was matched only by the hardness she showed his female patients, whom she referred to as his "daughters." During the ten years she had been with him, Irène had never failed in her devotion, a devotion that bordered on veneration. This suited Lamaze perfectly. Irène was useful to him. She knew how to keep quiet and drive smoothly, which let him do his reading in the car.

With a distraught expression Lamaze collapsed onto the backseat, biting his lip to keep from retching. He could not believe he was leaving Bluets for the last time, saying good-bye to a major part of his life, as well as to the cause that had guided it. He loved the working-class neighborhood where the hospital was located—the cabarets and back alleys; the air always seemed saturated with the smell of sweat and warm wine. It brought to mind the novels of Emile Zola and Balzac, and especially those of detective writer Georges Simenon, who had situated the apartment of his hero, Inspector Maigret, not far from the hospital.

For someone who had spent his childhood in the provincial Lorraine region, Paris was endlessly fascinating. As a boy, wandering along the banks of the Moselle River, Lamaze had dreamed of Paris, feeding his imagination on the writings of those who he thought best evoked it. When he had come to Paris, he continued his wanderings, book in hand, until he knew the city better than most Parisians.

The car began to move. Lamaze sat silently in the back. A little farther down the road a group of union activists were emerging from the Metal Workers' headquarters. When they saw Lamaze's car, they went out into the street to try to make it stop. Looking out the car window, Lamaze recognized some of them. Leading them was a little man in a gray overcoat; as the car slowed, he stepped forward to greet Lamaze. My grandfather paid him no attention. This man, thought Lamaze, was the archetypal bureaucrat—with his watery eyes and a sweaty, obsequious handshake. He told Irène not to stop the car.

His ears were ringing. To control his rage, he closed his eyes and began reciting passages from Victor Hugo's *The Legend of the Centuries* aloud. Lamaze had always believed that Hugo's poetry exerted therapeutic powers once you let its music seep into you. It didn't work this time. The depressing thought that he was finished, once and for all, was too overwhelming. The coup de grace had been the Lunet Report—a sterile catalog of numbers that had damned everything they had achieved at the hospital.

And now Lamaze was bitter. He had fought hard for six long years, staving off the growing hate unleashed by his theories about childbirth pain. He had dared to put himself in opposition to the Bible and to centuries of unquestioned obstetric practice. When he had been dragged before the Medical Board—abandoned by most of his colleagues—he had not given up the fight. And just when he believed that he had achieved victory for his method, and that at long last he could begin to relax, the bureaucrats and politicians had delivered their fatal blow.

Lamaze focused on the back of Irène's head. Her hair was pulled severely back into a bun, but on the nape of her neck fine curls of an ash gray had eluded the hairpins. Lamaze couldn't take his eyes off this infant down; it seemed so out of place on an ex-con. His eyes filled with tears. What a weak old man he had become. He felt bloated, his breath heavy and thickened by too many troubles, too many rich meals.

He had never fit in. The village girls of his youth had rejected him for rougher types; he had played the soldier during World War I, but always felt like a man without a country; he had never become chummy with the doctor crowd—all they had wanted to talk about was taxes and salaries; he felt out of place with the Communists, though he worked with them.

"Dumb as a baby doctor." He had heard that expression often enough. Perhaps he should have pursued other goals. But he had been determined to be a giver of life. It had offered him a way of changing the world. Moreover, his work on painless childbirth was but part of a far greater project. He had believed that changing the experience of labor and abolishing pain would lead to other changes in the way we live and behave.

Now he felt as if his dreams were turning to ashes. Lamaze took a deep breath and tried to slow his breathing, but he felt as if he were turning into jelly. This had to be part of what his friend Joseph Lévy-Valensi had dubbed the "dispossession syndrome": "If boiling water could feel its molecules flying apart, it would have the feeling of dispossession."

Drained, dispossessed, he gave in to the rhythms of the moving car until they reached the corner of rue du Dragon, where Irène dropped him off. He needed to walk a little, but the air dazed him and he found it difficult to move. No one on the street. In front of Alard's grocery store, a pushcart salesman was waiting for the next customer, browning some fritters and fries in blackish oil. Moving clumsily from his old war wound, Lamaze dragged himself home.

The courtyard of 21 rue du Dragon was filled with fig trees, acacias, and chestnuts—it was a haven of peace. Louise had originally chosen the apartment because it was located on the ground floor and looked out onto the trees in the backyard. Here they had lived since 1920. And there had been happy years. He knew what a miracle it was that a cultured, educated woman had become the wife—or rather, the Girl Friday—of a vulgar, bawdy peasant, an atheist whose only marriage present had been a case of syphilis he had gotten from a whorehouse in Nancy. He had never looked too deeply into the mystery of her devotion, what it was that lay behind her perpetual mask of serenity. Louise had always been there for him, always been discreet. Yet she knew how to set him straight when he had gone too far.

Why, Lamaze wondered, had she chosen today of all days to leave him by himself, taking off to the country with her daughter? He entered the empty apartment with a heavy heart. Everything was tidy and smelled of mothballs. He didn't touch the breakfast that Louise had left for him, and went through a series of dark, narrow rooms to his office. Crammed with books, the room looked more like a scholar's lair than a doctor's office. Every kind of book was there—philosophy, history, fiction, medical treatises. Lamaze believed that when it came to books there should be no boundaries. He loved losing himself in this vast junkyard of thought, and he considered a first edition of the works of Saint Bonaventure no more valuable than the dog-eared paperbacks of his beloved Kipling. Like the women he had loved, each book had its particular smell, and before undressing, he enjoyed a last whiff of the yellowed pages of Joachim Du Bellay's *The Re-grets*—about the fall of Rome—a gift from his grandfather.

His movements were slow; he needed to save his breath. He was nauseated, and a dull pain hammered in his head. He haphazardly tossed his clothing on a chair and moved heavily toward the couch. In the mirror he saw his image: a heavy, aging man with sagging shoulders and a receding chin. So this was what remained of the intense young crackpot who had once dreamed of remaking the world. Where was that titanic energy now?

He would have a beautiful funeral. He could already see the courtyard strewn with wreaths and bouquets. Telegrams from all over the world. Fresh flowers put on his grave every year—until people forgot. He swallowed some bismuth and went to bed. He was a man of habit; he waited patiently for sleep, and it came.

Chronicle of a Death Foretold

I TRIED TO SEE DR. VELLAY AGAIN. His secretary told me he had left for Latin America to give a series of lectures. She would let me know when he got back.

Disappointed, I still kept following up leads. Thanks to Jacques Caron, I met René Angelergues, with whom Jacques had worked at the Enfants-Malades children's hospital. Lamaze had asked this cultivated, perceptive man to fill the post of neuropsychiatrist at Bluets in 1953. Angelergues had thought highly of my grandfather. He confirmed what I had suspected: Lamaze suffered from depression, made worse by conflicts with authorities. He also explained that the medical program at Bluets had been part of a propaganda campaign waged by the Communist Party—part of their fight to empower the working class. Lamaze had never been able to buy into such a rationale; little wonder that he was crushed by the system and that his most important work was cut short, thwarted by ideology and politics.

The next person I met had arrived at the same grim conclusion. François Le Guay maintained that his dismissal from Bluets had not left him bitter; he said, rather matter-of-factly, that he had been the victim of "Stalinist reasoning." A militant unionist but not a member of the Communist Party, Le Guay had assumed financial management of Bluets in 1952. To him, my grandfather was a man of ethics wholeheartedly devoted to his profession. Lamaze, he thought, belonged to a different time; he was unprepared for the take-no-prisoners approach to politics. Giving me what seemed like a sly smile, Le Guay suggested I talk to other members of Lamaze's staff who had been victims of the great purge. They would, he thought, have a great deal to tell me.

I felt I was going in circles. I still could not get hold of Vellay, though the list of questions I wanted to ask him was getting longer every day. I wondered if the other members of Lamaze's staff—with names like Hersilie, Bourrel, Muldworf, Alexandre, Lacour, Vermorel—were still alive. I had been told that the daughter of Pierre Rouquès was living somewhere in central France. No one knew where. And no one knew under what name.

Assisted by the current management of Bluets I was able to meet with former members of the hospital administrative team. They came to see me as a group, were clearly moved by the idea of meeting "the doctor's granddaughter." A coincidence of genetics had suddenly placed me on a pedestal. I felt a combination of pride and embarrassment. They were all past the age of retirement; the battle for the Lamaze Method had taken place during their prime. This made their memories of the time that much more powerful. In their eyes, Lamaze had been a sort of warm, debonair "daddy" who had taught them the meaning of solidarity and made each of them feel an equal member of a team, each with his place and role. Indeed, for the Lamaze Method to have any chance of success with women, the entire staff had needed to participate, from the switchboard operator to the cleaning lady. One stern expression or rude remark could make the pregnant woman anxious, ruining months of preparation.

"There will never be another Dr. Lamaze," one told me as they left. I found I had tears in my eyes while I watched these loyal guardians go.

The next morning, I got a message that Vellay would expect me back at the House of Glass at two that afternoon. When I arrived, the secretary invited me in, then asked me to wait for a moment. I was trembling with anticipation. I had so many questions to ask Vellay. Several moments later, the secretary came back alone, carrying a file.

"The doctor can't see you, but he asked me to give you this," she told me, holding out a blue folder.

Somehow this theatrical touch did not surprise me. The House of Glass was designed to convey illusions—it is all about twists and turns, false transparencies. I left with the file and went to a café, which was filled with students from the Institute of Political Science, and began to acquaint myself with what was in the blue folder. Vellay had reconstructed my grandfather's activities before his death—hour by hour—by means of documents, letters, and press articles. I had the uncanny impression of reading the report of a trial whose outcome had been decided in advance:

Dear Mademoiselle,

I'm sorry to tell you that I couldn't get the notes your grandfather took when he was in Russia. My wife is still looking for the documents about our wrangles with the Medical Board. However, I have found some information that might prove useful to you.

The Lunet File

Considerations on the measures to take to balance the financial management of the maternity hospital.

This study is based on three initial principal ideas:

1. The maternity hospital should not be showing a deficit.
2. Since it is not possible to locate supplementary resources (we cannot ask the women who give birth here to participate financially), there is an absolute necessity to cut expenses.
3. The proposed measures of economy should not, as a whole, appreciably reduce the quality of care at the maternity hospital. . . .

THIS WAS FOLLOWED with a note by Vellay: "This report goes on with twenty pages of denunciation, aimed at eliminating the key posts in obstetrics and effectively destroying the work of your grandfather. I'll cite just a few passages in which the hypocritical zeal of a model bureaucrat permits a few crumbs of bravura":

The job of secretary (Cuvilliers) to the Painless Delivery Project was created in June 1953.

The job consists of:

a. Scheduling lessons for women with the obstetrician (notifying them).
b. Managing statistics on the results obtained from the Painless Childbirth Method.
c. Gathering reports written by the women after delivery (4 times a day).
d. Meeting and managing "doctors and midwives-in-training" and acting as secretary to the obstetricians.

In addition to attending to these practical duties, Cuvilliers plays an important role in contributing:

• To development (or rather, the support of the team in the Painless Childbirth Group).
• To the effective functioning of the union branch for which he serves as secretary (which takes up a good part of his time).

However, this job is not indispensable.
    The four tasks listed above could also be done by:

a. The supervisor of the maternity ward.
b. The supervisor of the health center.

There was another notation made by Vellay: "The list of executions was long, and good intentions bloomed. But the conclusion really showed its true colors."

All the proposed measures will bring significant changes to the maternity hospital, even from the point of view of its basic operating principles, but it is not possible to cut expenses merely by dealing with details.

The concept of the maternity hospital itself must now be put under discussion. Was it just to think of it as the pilot hospital at the beginning of the Painless Childbirth Project? Was it just to institute such exhaustive research and to take charge, at our expense, of instructing so many doctors and midwives from France and other countries? That is what must now be put under discussion.

a. Painless childbirth is now a reality in large sectors of the medical and scientific world, and although the battle for it is not over, it has, essentially, been won.

b. We no longer have a reason to consider ourselves as the current and future maternity hospital for teaching painless childbirth.

c. If most of the doctors and midwives who came to the workshops at the beginning were interested in the development of painless childbirth, most who come now do so more out of personal interest.

Thus, there is no reason to make the Metal Workers maternity hospital continue to be the only hospital playing the role of a "laboratory" for painless childbirth.

Vellay: "This sentence destroyed your grandfather. Caught in the trap, he tried to put up a struggle, as testified by the letter he sent on March 4 to a high-ranking leader of the Party."

My dear friend,

Tuesday evening there will be a meeting that will include representatives of the United Federation of Metal Workers and the medical commission. Would it be possible for Benoît Frachon to be at that meeting, the goal of which is to discuss issues recently raised? Concerning this matter, I continue to be amazed that serious decisions putting the very existence of the maternity division and the hospital have been taken by the Metal Workers union without prior medical consultation. What is more, I am quite disturbed by rumors concerning the replacement of Le Guay, who, as director, has been of enormous assistance in making the hospital what it is today.

On other occasions, I have come close to handing in my resignation. I did not do so, in the interests of the Painless Childbirth Method and the Pierre Rouquès Health Center. Were it to come to my attention that the work we have accomplished in five years, work which has brought the maternity hospital international prestige, was being endangered by the decisions of the Federation of Metal Workers, I could not remain at the head of the maternity hospital, and I would judge it my duty to publicly state the reasons for my departure.

Sincerely yours,
Dr. F. Lamaze

P.S. I am sending one copy of this letter to Benoît Frachon and another to the medical commission.

Vellay: "On Wednesday, March 6, Dr. Lamaze passed away. His death was a stroke of luck for the Party. In reaction, my father-in-law took up his pen and expressed all his contempt to the secretary general, André Lunet."

Dear Comrade,

Dr. Lamaze died this morning.

Lamaze was my oldest friend, and in this capacity I have been part of his struggles, so I was informed by him of the events of these last few days.

In 1951, upon his return from a trip to the U.S.S.R., this man gave up a secure position and peace of mind to proclaim his belief in the efficacy of painless childbirth. He then saw the majority of those who called themselves friends distance themselves from him, and even rise up against him. He was brought before the Medical Board and abandoned by most of the officials, but at Bluets, in the Metal Workers' hospital, where our mutual friend Pierre Rouquès got him a position, something like a new family was born. This new position allowed him to put his magnificent method within reach of the French working class, and eventually all the women of France. And this method was enriched thanks to his research and to his perseverance as a man of the people.

And at the moment when he thought he had the right to a certain moral and intellectual peace of mind, he found that he was being personally attacked—even though, thanks to him, the maternity hospital had become the most famous in the entire world. And now he was being attacked, not by the government officials, but by whose whom he had considered his comrades in the struggle, by the Metal Workers union, which owed so much to him. This is to inform you of your part in the responsibility for his death, which occurred a few hours after a discussion that neither his body nor his sensibility could bear.

Since you may not be aware of your responsibility regarding this, I consider it my duty as a man, friend, and Communist to place it before your conscience.

With sadness,
Jean Dalsace

Vellay: "André Lumet did not waste any time answering. His response is dated March 7."

Sir,

We write you in the name of the Federation of Metal Workers of Paris, who are proud to have helped and supported our friend Dr. Lamaze with all our strength in the noble and difficult mission that he undertook after his return from the U.S.S.R.: allowing mothers to give life joyously.

We write you in the name of those for whom Dr. Lamaze renewed his friendship and trust the day before his death.

We are pained, as are all metal workers and all women, by the cruel loss and premature death of our great friend. The day before he died, we were still working with him on projects for a defense campaign for the Painless Childbirth Method.

We are proud that Dr. Lamaze placed his trust in us until his final moments, knowing that we would help complete his life's work, as he stated in his writings and in the numerous lectures he gave in France and throughout the world.

We know, as he himself said so often, and as Mme Lamaze has repeated, that he was very disturbed by the treacherous attacks against him on the part of certain reactionary members of the medical community who were frightened by the light of truth Dr. Lamaze brought back from the Soviet Union.

We also know that certain people who were jealous of his friendship with us and of the distinguished role he played in the maternity division of the Pierre-Rouquès Health Center—which is one of the most stunning gifts to society by the Parisian Metal Workers—plotted to turn him away from us, but that Dr. Lamaze's superior honesty and devotion eventually overcame all such intrigues.

In the face of such friendship and reciprocal trust between a man of science and a union of workers, forged by a shared fight, how could the monstrous ignominy of your letter, whose basis is beyond the limits of the imaginable, stand up?

How dare you suggest that we personally attacked our friend, whose role at the head of our maternity hospital was so valuable to us!

Permit us, as workers, to tell you that your words are an outrage to the memory of the man you claim was your friend.

Permit us, as union activists, to tell you that the titles with which you come decorated, in addressing a letter to a union organization, do not in our eyes contribute the slightest value to your letter.

What counts is not the titles one claims or proclaims, but merit, rectitude, and dignity.

Your letter is not inspired by these qualities, which forces us to inform you that your attitude only serves the enemies of the workers and their organizations.

It is our turn to ask you to face your conscience: we hope this will help you to understand that the Metal Workers consider your attitude an insult.

Secretary General
André Lunet

Vellay: "Jean Dalsace didn't let it rest at that. On March 12, he sent Raymond Guyot the following letter":

Dear Comrade,

I have sent you a copy of the letter to Lunet. Enclosed is the answer I received.

I have no intention of continuing the correspondence. But given the injurious insinuations and untruths contained in his letter, which put my honor into question, I am asking you to arrange a face-to-face confrontation with Lunet, in the presence of one of the physicians who would have attended the meeting on March 5.

I'm convinced that you will understand my reasons for disturbing you. What Lunet has written demands a personal meeting, which, with all my heart, I am requesting you to arrange.

In brotherhood,
Jean Dalsace

Vellay: "Raymond Guyot organized the meeting for Wednesday, March 13, at 6 P.M. The next day, Dalsace resigned his membership from the Communist Party with much fanfare. The press got wind of what would become 'the Lamaze affair.' It was the Communist Party's newspaper, *L'Humanité,* that lit the fuse. After having devoted its front page to the father of painless childbirth, there followed an article by André Wurmser, accusing the conservative newspaper *Le Figaro* of silence on the issue. On March 11, the editors of *Le Figaro* retorted:

COMMUNIST INDECENCY

L'Humanité and the organs of the Communist Party have paid homage to the work of Dr. Fernand Lamaze, who was responsible for spreading throughout France the practice of painless childbirth, based on the work of Pavlov. They are not the only ones to be doing so, and the recent articles by M. Wurmser, who has denounced the supposed silence of *Le Figaro* on the issue, is particularly vile. On the very day of his death, it has used the accomplishments and devotion of a man who dedicated himself wholeheartedly to his profession, and without ever engaging in radical politics, for its own propaganda purposes.

M. Wurmser would have done better to enlighten his readers about the way in which the Federation of Metal Workers, one of the bastions of the Communist Party, showed its gratitude to Dr. Lamaze. The day before his death, he was subjected to the most vicious attacks from union representatives, who used the budget deficit of their hospital, where Dr. Lamaze and his colleagues practiced his method, to reject his practice as too costly, and to dismiss the hospital director, M. Le Guay, who, it should be noted, had justifiably protested Soviet repression in Hungary. Following a violent argument in which it became clear to Dr. Lamaze that he was being disowned, he had a stroke. He died the next morning of a heart attack.

Vellay: "The fight had begun, and there would be no holds barred. The Fraternal Union of Metal Workers demanded the right to reply to the editorial in *Le Figaro,* maintaining that 'Dr. Lamaze suffered no personal attack and his illness occurred neither before nor after the meeting of the hospital's medical administration.'

"*Le Figaro* published their reply but did not back down from its accusations, 'based on information from the most reliable sources.' Doubt festered in people's minds. The publication *Combat* interviewed me and used the headline: 'Dr. Lamaze Died Because of His Detractors.'

"There's no sense in continuing. You have all the evidence in hand. To conclude, I will merely cite the moving article Henri-François Rey wrote about your grandfather for *France Observateur.*"

The last years of his life were full of worry. This man, who embodied kindness and loyalty, refused to play sordid games that no longer had anything to do with his quest to liberate humanity. This man, who belonged to the left out of a sense of generosity, could not bring himself to accept that there were those claiming to represent the left who lacked any generosity whatsoever. Fortunately, he still had his profession, a passion for mastering it, his research, his unending search for new techniques. But something in him was beginning to give out.

Not long ago, at Bluets Hospital, which had been his professional home, the union, led by the Communists, decided without consulting him to modify the organization of the hospital. Their decision was to distance themselves from Lamaze's principal collaborators and curtail in large measure his basic activities. This was a grievous blow for him. He fought them, debated them, and attacked them, during a raucous meeting, at the end of which he was stricken by a stroke. He died of a heart attack the next day.

Unlike *Le Figaro,* we do not argue that Dr. Lamaze was indirectly murdered by the Communists. We are only pointing out the bizarre attitude of those who unscrupulously appropriated his work yet came close to taking away his means to pursue it. And yet, somehow, this didn't prevent them from devoting three columns in *L'Humanité* to the memory of the very person they had tried to get rid of the day before.

Such methods are disgusting, and it is quite probable that Dr. Lamaze felt deeply revolted. His life was that of the "honest man," in the old sense of the term. He was a humanist, a genuine man of culture, who placed nothing above intellectual honesty and lucidity. He was a deeply civilized man whose taste for and whose sense of human relationships was acute, and who was ready at the age of sixty to jeopardize his career, comfort, and even his well-being in order to devote himself to work he believed was just and effective, which it was.

In France his name will always be associated with that body of work that has contributed, more than any other, to the liberation of women. And his exemplary life clearly illustrates what happens to those who struggle to retain their integrity and honesty. Those sorts of attributes are rarely pardoned.

Epilogue

The Communist Party would never reveal the true nature of its disagreement with Lamaze. They covered it with flowers at his funeral, which took place on March 9, 1957. The flowers spilled out into the courtyard of his home—wreaths from the Communist Party and the Federation of Metal Workers, garlands of mauve lilacs from the Soviet embassy. The following year, the Union of French Women organized a campaign to empower local chapters to suggest town squares, small public gardens, and maternity hospitals that might be named after Lamaze. One Party newspaper launched a subscription drive to finance a marble bust of the doctor that would be given to his family.

While going through the archives at Bluets, I happened on a file entitled *Campaign in Memory of the Death of Lamaze.* Inside were a number of press clippings, the minutes of the international conferences on the Lamaze Method, and several letters sent by Albert Carn to my grandmother. In one letter, dated March 3, 1958, he informed her that on Thursday, March 6, at 12:30 P.M., the employees and doctors at Bluets would be meeting in the hall on the third floor in order to pay homage to her husband. On Saturday, March 8, a delegation was sent to his grave at Grosrouvre.

The following year Carn again sent his troops instructions to place flowers on Lamaze's grave. This gesture brought together the administrative staff of the Communist Party, the Union of French Women, the Syndicated Union, the Fraternal Union, the Confederation of Workers, the Syndicated Union of Workers, the Metal Workers, and the director of Saint-Denis Hospital. It was the final great blaze of Communist propaganda. I find their persistence in enshrining the memory of a man whose death they had precipitated somehow poignant. The question is whether this persistence stemmed from guilt or from an awareness that it was the end of an era.

Months passed. I still had not answered that question. My mother was released from the hospital; Jacques Caron died; I made several visits to the cemetery in Grosrouvre, where my father is buried next to his father-in-law and Louise. The Lamaze file is still missing a few pieces, though now and again new leads open up. A close friend in the secret service is looking for traces of my grandfather in their archives; he believes Lamaze would have been put under surveillance because of his Communist connections. I have a cousin who is a professor at the university in Montpellier and the author of a fascinating book on obstetrics and the Cold War. She tells me that she will introduce me to others who were at Bluets Hospital and might have new information. At some point I will meet with the widow of the former mayor of Saint-Denis, who had been a faithful friend of my grandfather's.

Looking on the Internet I located more than a thousand entries for Lamaze, most of them created in the United States, where a brand of toys has even been named after him. There my grandfather's techniques are called the Lamaze Method. Not in France. Perhaps this is proof of our tendency toward understatement. Only the bare bones of the original method remain: the cost of six classes in "preparation for childbirth" that are reimbursed by French government insurance. The general consensus is that the epidural has made any other technique of dealing with the fear and suffering of women in labor superfluous. And yet I believe that Lamaze's campaign for painless childbirth is more relevant today than ever. Perhaps one day a medical historian will provide a detailed look at how this crucial period prefigured the reproductive battles that were to come, and provide some answers.

As for me, I have tried to get at the truth in my own way—by using the notebooks and diaries and photographs—though I would not conclude that the truth of fiction prevails over reality. All that I can do is write "my" book, and for me a sentence like "Fernand Lamaze left the delivery room with bloody hands" brings him to life.

I found a strange press clipping among my grandfather's notebooks. It was a brief article from *Le Figaro* about a mass suicide of rats in the Chinese region of Xinjang. Dozens of thousands of rats were found floating on lakes and rivers, "an expression of sadness on their faces." This old scrap of paper haunted him, and it haunts me. I keep going back to the way I had imagined, and worded, his final day.

On Wednesday, March 6, in the morning, Lamaze came home. The house was empty. He went into the kitchen to drink a glass of bismuth, then decided to go to bed. He was still agitated. He regulated his breathing, the way he had taught so many women to do, and summoned all his memories. One cannot depart without taking stock. He remembered his childhood. He remembered the thick eiderdown quilts and the perfumes he made with the baker's daughter by crushing rose petals. Then he saw Lison, Edward Larquin, Betty Paxton, Jean Le Bey Taillis, Lévy-Valensi, and Emile Gutmann, who had a flower of blood on his chest but seemed to be smiling. Louise and her lashless eyes, Anne-Marie at the window in Grosrouvre. The images sped by more and more rapidly, until they blended together and then disappeared. He waited. He knew what was coming; all he needed was patience. He recognized an odor, the very specific and slightly nauseating odor of the placenta. Then a cry pierced his ears. It was at that instant that he closed his eyes.

Suggested Reading

Arms, Suzanne. *Immaculate Deception II: Myth, Magic & Birth*. Berkeley, California: Celestial Arts, 1994.

Davis-Floyd, Robbie, and Carolyn Fishel Sargent. *Childbirth and Authoritative Knowledge: Cross-Cultural Perspectives*. Berkeley, California: University of California Press, 1997.

Davis-Floyd, Robbie E. *Birth As an American Rite of Passage*. Berkeley, California: University of California Press, 1993.

Karmel, Marjorie. *Thank You, Dr. Lamaze*. New York: Dolphin Press, 1965.

Lamaze, Fernand. *Painless Childbirth—Psychoprophylactic Method*. Chicago: Henry Regnery Company, 1970.

Marland, Hilary, and Anne Marie Rafferty. *Midwives, Society and Childbirth: Debates and Controversies in the Modern Period (Studies in the Social History of Medicine)*. New York: Routledge, 1997.

McGregor, Deborah Kuhn. *From Midwives to Medicine: The Birth of American Gynecology*. Piscataway, New Jersey: Rutgers University Press, 1998.

Murphy-Lawless, Jo. *Reading Birth and Death: A History of Obstetric Thinking*. Bloomington, Indiana: Indiana University Press, 1999.

Odent, Michael. *Birth Reborn*. Medford, New Jersey: Birth Works, 1994.

Savage, Beverly, and Diane Simkin. *Preparation for Birth: The Complete Guide to the Lamaze Method*. New York: Ballantine, 1987.

Wertz, Dorothy and Richard. *Lying-In: A History of Childbirth in America*. New Haven: Yale University Press, 1989.

Acknowledgments

I'd like to thank Dr. Pierre Vellay for his precious memories. He and his wife, Aline, opened their archives to me and helped me to illuminate some of the shadowy areas in my grandfather's life. I also thank René Angelergues, Yves Cachin, Emile Papiernick, Pierre Simon, and Guy Vermeil for their kindness and for helping me clarify certain medical (and nonmedical) aspects of my subject.

Thanks to all the women and men who so generously told me their stories: Chantal Chaudé de Silans, Marie-Jeanne Detoeuf, Agnès Devergie, Simonne Gillot, François Le Guay, Marianne Lellieuz, Reine and Gilberte Valensi, and the "elders" of the staff at Bluets. Thanks equally to Evelyne Vander Heym, the current director of the Pierre-Rouquès Hospital of Metal Workers, for her warm welcome.

And finally, thanks to my first readers, François Bourin and Claude Druand, and to those who knew how to give birth to this project, Isabelle and Laurent Laffont.

Index